Round Holes, Square Pegs and Pigeonholes

by Millie Malone Lill

This book is dedicated to all the polio survivors and other people with disabilities and their families who have read and enjoyed my ongoing columns in the Nebraska Polio Survivors Association's newsletter Gleanings, and my online newsletter Polio Perspective. Also, to those who bought my first book Hot Water, Orange Juice and Kids. Thank you from the bottom of my heart.

Round Holes, Square Pegs and Pigeonholes

For most of my life, I've been a misfit. If the Round Hole was big enough, I could sort of fit in, but there would be noticeable gaps on top, bottom and sides. In school, I was not teased or tormented because of my limp but I was only accepted in a limited sort of way. It was understood that certain things were not available to me. No one ever explained the why or wherefore of this, but I believed it. I just accepted the fact that while the other girls my age were swooning over the football players, or going out for cheer-leading or homecoming queen, I was expected to be a spectator. My mother also assured me that I was unacceptable as marriage material, so dating would be an exercise in futility. No one would ask me, anyhow, so it was moot.

As I got older, I noticed the before unseen gaps in the Round Hole around my square person. When a guy asked me to get married right out of high school, I accepted. I knew no one else would ever ask and that if I wanted a family, I better catch this train before it left the station. Although I got very good grades in school, college was out of the question. It was not even considered for me. I was only good enough for marriage, not for a career.

My marriage, fortunately, was a happy one. I loved being a mommy and I loved being a wife. I filled the gaps in the Round Hole with children, my own and as many of everyone else's as were available. We had a good team going, my husband, myself, and our three sons. Unfortunately, my husband's health failed him shortly after we married. His appendix ruptured and he nearly died. That was the first of eight separate times that I was told he would not make it. The eighth time arrived too soon and I was a widow at age 52.

I'd been given a computer by my Vocational Rehabilitation counselor and urged to learn to use it. I started classes at Western Iowa Tech, a community college about 10 miles from my farm. I fit in better there, despite the vast age difference between me and most of the other students, than I had in high school. I loved it. I learned a lot about computers and learned how to use the Internet.

The Internet! I did a search for Post Polio Syndrome and found an online support group. To my surprise, I found an unlimited number of Square Pegs! Here was the Square Hole I'd been looking for my whole life. No gaps, top, bottom, or sides. Nope. I fit in perfectly. I was accepted completely. The novelty of that nearly knocked my socks off.

Starting then, in 1996, I was part of what I've come to see as my polio family. No need to explain to them why I could not go dancing or hiking or stand in line for extended periods. They knew. They couldn't, either. My blood family might raise an eyebrow if I skipped a funeral because the church was not accessible, but my polio family didn't blink an eye.

Even my writing finally had an outlet. I wrote columns for Gleanings, the newsletter for the Nebraska Polio Survivors Association, and later I started doing an online polio newsletter. There were still times that people wanted to stuff me in a pigeonhole labeled INVALID, but I refused to stay there. No, just because I use a power chair does not mean that my mind doesn't work. And no, just because I can walk a little bit, it does not mean that I'm 'giving in' if I use my chair.

I am very much enjoying the Square Hole I live in now. I've wiggled around in it enough to round its edges as well as my own. It is neither Round nor Square at the moment, and it definitely is not a pigeon hole.

ALL ABOARD!

It's 3:00 AM. I stagger out of my bedroom, eyes squinting against the kitchen light. It's time to head for Omaha, a two hour drive away, to meet my train. My grandson helps me get my luggage in the van and drives me to the station, cheerful and un-bleary at this hour. I've chosen Amtrak because I can travel with my power chair right beside me. This will be my first trip on a train since I was a child.

The California Zephyr is a fun train and my fellow passengers are cheerful and friendly as the redcap rolls out the ramp and helps me get aboard. "Do you need another seat besides your wheelchair, ma'am?" he asks. "Because there are no more seats on this car. I could take you on down the line about 13 cars, if you need to transfer to a seat during this leg of your trip." Not wanting to be a bother, we PWDs (Persons With Disabilities) are so well trained that way, I decline his offer and spend the next 10 hours wishing I had been a pain in the butt instead of causing myself to have one. Mental note: 10 hours is too long to remain in my non-reclining, not very comfortable Jazzy. Further mental note: next wheelchair will be a more comfortable one.

I reach into one of the bags that festoon my chair like the packs on a prospector's donkey. There are snacks, beverages, a cross stitch project, books and my reading glasses in there. I came prepared. While making my reservations, I was told that a service attendant would happily bring me a menu from the dining car and bring my food to me. Ever the skeptic, I brought enough snacks to tide me over. The service attendant did show up once and I begged a psuedo-pillow off him and slept, after a fashion, for a few hours. That was the last I saw of the service attendant. Lunch was announced. People left to find food. I nibbled snacks and felt smug.

Around 4:00 PM, the train pulls into the Chicago station. It is huge. I'm so glad I have my power chair. While I can walk a little bit, I could never manage the several blocks from my car to the waiting area. I see a redcap coming into the waiting room, pulling a handcart piled high with bags. A smiling, vibrant woman tells him to be sure and come back and get her when her train leaves. He sees me in my chair and says. "I'll help you aboard at the same time, OK? You just stay here with Betty." The woman comes over to me, introduces herself and we decide to go have something from the food court. Odd how I always manage to meet someone interesting in the strangest places.

At last, the redcap arrives and we head for the car that will deliver me to Buffalo, where my friend Carolann will pick me up and take me to her home in St. Catharines, Ontario. Betty is put in a different car. I feel as if I've parted from a long time friend. After much maneuvering, the redcap comes to the logical conclusion that there is no way to get me into the handicapped car because a pillar is blocking access to the door. We move to another car, further down the line. Once again, I am grateful that I have the power chair. I could never do the amount of walking involved in this project. I have a car almost to myself on this leg. I am in the back of the car, next to the bathroom. This time, I transfer to an "attendant chair" that is thoughtfully provided for those of us who have attendants traveling with us. I find that the attendant chair does not recline as fully as the others and has no leg rest. Attendants must not be high on the priority list. My wheelchair, pulled up in front of the attendant seat makes a nice leg rest. I crunch up, using one of the railroad's tiny, flat noone-would-want-to-stealthis pillows and sleep as long as possible.

Dawn breaks over Lake Erie. If I were a morning person, or a person who had slept comfortably, or a person who awakens happy and bright-eyed, I would revel in the glory of the sight. I squint at it for a moment and go back to sleep. My train is still two hours from my destination.

Arrival at the Buffalo depot is very welcome. My friend is visible through the window, waiting for the train to stop so we can start our month long visit. At reservation time, I was told that if my chair was "less than 36" wide and less than 48" long" it would fit nicely. Wrong. My chair is about 25"x25" and turns in its own radius. I get stuck making the right turn out of the car. A slim young woman, perhaps the elusive service attendant, insists she can lift this 250 lb. chair with me seated in it. Much to my surprise, she does.

What a trip. It wasn't faster than the bus, but I could move around more than in the bus. It wasn't faster than flying either, having taken 23 hours, but my chair was safely beside me at all times. The price, with my handicap discount and the special that was being run to celebrate Amtrak's 30th year of business, was very attractive. In spite of a few glitches, I believe I will travel this way again.

My friend and I drive off to her home in St. Catharines, Ontario where we will do some sight seeing, some shopping and a lot of laughing.

And the Beat Goes On...

Last year, I had the opportunity to pass along my used Jazzy power chair to a man in Michigan who had COPD. This was part of my Recycled Wheels of Love project. I got an email message asking me to contact his wife today. Dave had passed on. I only met Dave on the phone, but he seemed like such a nice man. I had talked to his wife Ann a few times, too. After accepting my condolences on her loss, Ann told me her plans for the Jazzy. She would like to let another member of her family, a young man, use the chair and when he replaces it or doesn't need it, she would like to donate it to her local Senior Center. Then, she told me, she'd like to start another branch of Recycled Wheels of Love.

To know that I have not only been able to improve Dave's life a little bit, but to know that the help is being passed along...I don't mind telling you, it brought tears to my eyes. How often does a person get a chance to make a difference in someone else's life? Maybe oftener than we know. Anyway, I was so touched by this that I had to pass it on.

In Dave's last days, his family rallied around him and their mother and took turns caring for him. That kind of love spreads, as can be seen by their wishing to give others the joy that little wheelchair gave Dave.

My father was right, as he so often was, when he said, "Everything is better when you share."

Christmas Memories

Christmas in a large family started a tradition that continues to this day. My husband was one of ten children. When our children were very young, it was decided that his family was too large to expect his mother to host Christmas every year. So we started with the oldest sibling and took turns, each year moving down the list to the next younger sibling. Since his mother's birthday was on Christmas Eve and was always celebrated with a soup supper, this meant that my children spent their Christmas holidays at other people's homes.

Determined to have our own celebration, I began making homemade chicken and noodles and inviting my parents to our home on the Sunday before Christmas. Our children would open their gifts that night and would have time to enjoy their toys before being whisked off to their cousins' homes.
No packages could be opened until the table was cleared from supper. The twinkle in my father's eyes as he declared that he wanted "just a little more" and the accompanying groans from my impatient children were all a part of the festivities. By the time Dad had satisfied his appetite, my sons were fairly dancing to get at those packages.

My husband is gone, my father is gone, many of the aunts and uncles are also gone. Our traditional chicken soup supper, however, remains. It has been moved to Christmas Eve so that my sons will have Christmas Day to spend with their own children or with their in-laws. Each year I take a snapshot of each of my sons with their families, one with me and my sons, and one with me and all my grandchildren. This year, Jordan, my first great grandchild joins the fun. And the beat goes on.

Chicken and Noodle Soup

5 lbs. chicken parts (I use hindquarters)
water to cover
salt, pepper, garlic, curry powder to taste (I find the smell of

boiling chicken somewhat offensive, but with the spices added, it smells great)
3 packages Kluski type egg noodles

Boil till the chicken is tender. Remove from the pot and cool the chicken till you can remove the skin and bones. If I have time, I refrigerate the broth and remove the fat that forms on the top. Put the meat back into the broth, bring to a boil and add the noodles. Cook till the noodles are tender. Serve in large bowls to the accompaniment of children giggling and Christmas carols playing, babies underfoot and much love.

CURING VS HEALING

There is a difference between being 'cured' and being 'healed.' Being cured means your illness is gone. Being healed means you are now whole. Are you with me so far? Then let's apply this to PPS. It is incurable, so curing is not gonna happen. Healing? I think we can do that. I think we have done that!

Let's use myself as an example. I no longer have polio, so in that sense I guess I'm cured. However, I'm left with PPS so, in that sense, I am not cured. But am I whole? I think I am. Can I do whatever I want to do? Yes and no. Many times I can do it, but the cost is prohibitive in terms of repercussions. For instance, if a light bulb goes, I can climb on a chair or stepladder and replace it. Chancy, because my hip is unreliable and so are my legs. Change that sentence to this: If a light bulb blows, can I get it replaced? Oh, put it that way and the answer is yes. I call our maintenance man or, before I had access to a maintenance man, I could call one of my kids, grandkids, or neighbors. The result as far as the light bulb is concerned is the same.

I could be bitter about not being able to dance, being tired all the time, not being able to be spontaneous. If I felt that way, while the polio is cured, I would not be healed. But I can still dance, if I find the right partner, one who is willing to stand in one spot and sway to the music or take a risk and dance with me in my power chair. As for being tired, I can take a nap whenever I want, sleep in as late as I like, and as far as planning ahead, I did that before PPS, too. So, looking at it that way, I am healed.

My children and grandchildren grew up with a disabled mother. No one gave it a thought. They were taught to offer help when they saw the need for it. My sons are tall...well, taller than my 5'2"...so they willingly got things for me that I couldn't reach. They did not expect me to suddenly become 6' tall, they just accepted that this was Mom and nothing wrong with that. They accepted my disability in the same way. If I couldn't do it, they could. If they couldn't do it, perhaps I could. We were a team. My grandchildren have also accepted me. My youngest grandson and I frequently went for 'walks' when we lived close together. He walked, I rode in my power chair. The dog went with us and none of us thought that I was not whole. I am whole. So are you. We don't need a faith healer to put his hands on our heads and pronounce it to the congregation. We can just accept that we are healed.

If we can accept ourselves as is, if we can remember that everyone has some limitations, we can be healed. I can't run, but my friend who can run cannot write a column on PPS. I can do that, but I can't sing. (I sing like a bird, but unfortunately, that bird is a crow.)
Everyone has something they cannot do. Everyone. The trick is to find that which we can do and go with it. Adapt. Accept ourselves as the imperfect human beings that we all are. Give ourselves credit for being survivors. We lived through polio when many did not. We are here, we can thrive, we are healed.

CUTE, OR NOT SO MUCH?

To many people, this may seem trivial. Perhaps it is, but I find it very annoying and I'm betting you do, too. When my friend and I are out toodling around in our power chairs, people say we are cute. My friend sees it as a compliment, but I see it as condescending and inappropriate.

Cute is for puppies, kittens, and children. I am a senior citizen and I have no desire to compete with the aforementioned group in a cute-a-thon. Oh, make no mistake, I like being told I am attractive, pretty, or that I look good for my age. OK, I'll get real, not that last one so much. It's better than being called cute, though.

"Cute" implies that we are more decorative than useful. Since I am not all that decorative, it puts my usefulness status at a very low ebb. I don't appreciate that. Being seen as cute makes me feel trivialized. Not important. Too helpless to be any good for anything. A cartoon, perhaps.

We polio survivors have been through a lot. Can you imagine a military veteran enjoying being called cute? Don't think so. He/she has served our country and should be treated with respect. We polio survivors have struggled, too, defied death in many cases, have contributed greatly to the common good. It was because of us that the ADA came into effect. We were the first group of disabled people to survive and thrive. We are not "cute."

No one who knows me at all will see me as stuffy or prim. I enjoy a good laugh, but I don't like feeling like the butt of a joke. Like all of us, I've endured surgeries, casts, braces, walkers, crutches and The Dreaded Power Chair. My disability does not define me, nor does it make me "less than."
When people think of me as cute, they seem to think it is OK to talk down to me, stand too close to me, pat me on the

shoulder/head even if they do not know me, or dismiss me as an unimportant member of society. I'm seen as no longer relevant. My intellect is judged by the fact that I am in a chair. Maybe some people sit on their brains, but I'm not one of them.

We are many things: parents, teachers, accountants, grandparents, writers, sisters, brothers...the list goes on and on. What we are not is "cute." And if I'm called cute one more time, I'm going to hold my breath till I turn blue! That will show them!

DEAR MS CONDUCT

Dear Ms. Conduct: I need some pointers on etiquette. What is the proper way to let someone know they have parked illegally in a handicapped zone? Disgruntled in Denison

Dear Disgruntled: The correct way to deal with this is to go inside the store, crawling on all fours if necessary (because there were no handicapped spots left, were there?) and report to the store manager. This should not take more than half an hour and you should still have enough energy left to crawl back to the car waaaaaaay on the other side of the parking lot and drive home. It's nice to have a cell phone along so you can call the kids and have them stand with the door open so you can get back in your house before you croak.

Dear Ms. Conduct: My husband took me out for my birthday to the nicest restaurant in town. However, once we were situated at the table with my wheelchair in place, the waitress spoke only to my husband, asking him "And what will She have?" without even looking at me. How should I have handled this? Hungry in Hannibal

Dear Hungry: This is a problem that comes up now and then. The problem, of course, is that when seated in a wheelchair you automatically become invisible to anyone over 3' tall. A friend of mine was in this same situation and she just tugged on the waitress' apron till she caught her attention. Then she motioned to the woman to be seated. When the waitress was seated, my friend asked her if she could hear. The waitress nodded "Yes. " Then my friend asked if she could speak. "Of course, " was the reply. "Then why do you assume I can neither speak nor hear if I am seated?" was my friend's retort, given with a sweet smile. The waitress blushed and took my friend's order.

Dear Ms. Conduct: I have recently gone into a wheelchair and now I'm worried that men will not be attracted to me anymore. Is there anything I can do to hang onto my sexuality? Lonely in Laramie

Dear Lonely: Remember to look your best when you go out in your wheelchair. I like to wear brightly colored clothing because it makes me feel pretty and cheerful. Fix your hair and put on makeup. Wear a smile, as that is your most important accessory. And when you are in a store or the mall and spot a good-looking man, you might want to nudge him with your chair just in back of the knees. As he lands in your lap, smile prettily and introduce yourself.

Dear Ms. Conduct; I am married to a polio survivor. Her doctor has told her to pace, but she insists on doing everything herself. How can I help her without making her feel helpless or worse yet, biting my head off? She is very independent! Worried in Wisconsin

Dear Worried: This is a toughy. You will have to watch her and let her do what she is still able to do, but step in before she does something foolish like climb on a rocking chair to reach a light bulb to change it. It has been known to happen.... I prefer not to mention how I know this. Polio survivors are very prickly about their independence, but if you wear one of those nice padded neck collars, it won't hurt as bad when she starts to gnaw on your jugular.

Ms. Conduct is available for consultation by writing to her in care of this paper or by visiting her website at http://www.yougottabekiddinghowgullibleareyouanyhow.com.

Dog Training

Every morning, I take my little dog for a 'walk.' She walks, I roll. Fiona is about the size of a sack of sugar in reality, but in her heart she is a Giant Great Dane. She reminds me of so many of my polio survivor friends. She may have limits but she will go right to the edge of them as often as possible. She will try so hard to pull me in my power chair, urging me to go faster than that.

However, Fiona has taught me some good lessons. She has been on a leash her entire life, just as we polio survivors are on our own Post Polio Leash. Therefore, she knows that there are certain things she can't do and she has developed strategies for such occasions. When she goes to check on her friend Brer Rabbit who lives under a large patch of spreading yew, she knows that there is a post to maneuver around. She knows how to go around an obstacle that prevents her from reaching her goal. If her leash does get tangled, she knows how to untangle it.

We could learn from this little dog. Well, I could. Maybe the rest of you are well aware of your Polio Leash. I keep forgetting it's there. Fiona knows that when she reaches the end of her leash, she has to back up or go a different direction. After all, there sits Momma, on the other end of that leash in a big power chair. Seven pounds of dog cannot pull over 300 Ibs. of Momma and chair combined. Sometimes she tries. Most often, she backs off in favor of something more doable.
Fiona has more sense than I do. I know that there's a big Momma on the end of my leash, too, but I try to fool myself into thinking I can change that if I try hard enough. If I just do it this way, or maybe if I do it that way...I don't learn as quickly as Fiona does.

Fiona knows enough to ask for help when she needs it, too. Mostly, like all of us, she is very independent, but faced with an empty water dish, she knows she needs help. She will then ask for me to fill it up. Seems simple, doesn't it Yet when I need something that I know I cannot do for myself, do I have enough sense to ask for help? Usually not. I'll still climb on my step stool, knowing full well that my bad hip will complain loudly and might, just for spite, dump me on the floor. I could wait until my nephew, who lives just down the hall, stops by and ask him to reach that high shelf. But do I? No. I don't want to bother him. Fiona has no compunction whatsoever in asking me to do little things for her. If her dog toy is under the couch, she shows me that she can't reach it and I use my grabber to get it for her.

Fiona is a lovely little companion and teacher. She will bring her toy to me so I can throw it and she can chase it. Sometimes she drops it on the floor in front of me. I tell her, "Fiona, I can't reach it." Then she will pick it up, put her front paws on my lap and deposit the toy (dog spit and all) on my knee. She is willing to train me, but I have to learn to cooperate. Someday maybe I'll accept my leash as graciously as she accepts hers.

Don't Give Me Your Attitude, I Have One of My Own

Raise your hand if you are tired of people making assumptions about you, your lifestyle, your financial status or your health, mental or physical, without truly even knowing you at all. That's what I thought. Most of us. OK, ALL of us!

I've been told that I was "far too retarded" (and those were the exact words, PC or not,) to raise a family. I raised three fine sons and took care of a husband whose health was never good besides. In spite of my seeming lack of gray matter, I managed a farm as well. I had help, of course, from those very sons and as much as could be managed from my husband, too. However, I was the one who bought and sold, wrote the checks, kept the books, and handled the budget.

On one occasion, I was in WalMart, looking for a poster one of the grandsons had requested as a birthday gift. I was in the store scooter and found there was no way to get to the display of posters. I knew one of the women working there and asked her why they'd put that display in such a difficult spot to reach. She looked me in the eye and told me that "people like you" were unlikely to be interested in such things.

Oh, that phrase really gets my goat. "People like you." Do you mean people who are short? People who have red hair? Perhaps you mean people who are not as rude as you are?? She was, of course, making assumptions based on the fact that I was not walking.

I've been told that I "look too good" to really need a wheelchair, that I need to "exercise off some of that fat" (this by a doctor, no less) and that I faked being able to walk so that I could smuggle my wheelchair into a senior housing complex that was already under the Fair Housing Act! Once I got over being angry about that last one, I stopped to wonder how one fakes being able to walk. I can walk, I don't have to fake it. I just can't walk very far or stand for very long without its causing me a lot of pain. Even so, anyone watching me walk would realize I don't do it well and certainly not gracefully.

I realize that PPS is an odd sort of thing. Other disabilities might be helped by working harder or exercising more, but PPS is made worse by this behavior. I have lived in this body for many years, and I know how it works and how it does not. No one else on the planet has this knowledge. Therefore, by informing myself, listening to my body and taking care of myself, I've made a very pleasant life without relying on strangers to advise me.

A casual acquaintance of many years once asked me why I always seem to be smiling and happy. The answer I gave him was that I live with me 24/7 and I don't want to live with a grouch. Actually, I usually am happy and that's why I smile. I have a lot for which to be grateful. I have friends who understand me, family who loves me, hobbies I enjoy, a decent living from the farm I worked so hard to keep.

What do we say to people who make these uncalled for assumptions? I don't know. Really, I just feel sad for them that they are so ignorant. I believe that living well is the best revenge. Also, I try to learn from the mistakes of others. It's unlikely I'll live long enough to make all of them myself, after all.

ROLL MODEL

Now that I am using my power chair more and more, I guess you could call me a roll model. I still think you would be better off doing what I say and not what I do, though. However, some people can learn from the mistakes of others and some must BE the others. Let's hope some of you can learn from the vast number of mistakes I have made. In order to help you do this, I have made the following list of Dos and Don'ts.

DON'T forget about your polio affected limb in a fit of decorating frenzy and step back off the coffee table (or the ladder, if you want to take ALL the sport out of it) onto a toe that has not functioned for over half a century and cannot be expected to do so now. As usual, I will plead the Fifth Amendment if asked how I gleaned this tidbit of info. Suffice it to say, even if that toe did work before, it sure won't now!

DO ask your grown children, spouse, siblings or neighbors to help with tasks that are now beyond your capabilities.

DON'T leave your power chair's speed control knob set to ZOOM when you are inside a building, especially if it is your home and you are in charge of making/ paying for repairs.

DO set the speed dial to Turtle as soon as you come inside. The cat you save may be your own.

DON'T wait until you are ready to step into the shower after an extended trip to see if the shower head has become clogged with lime through not being used for 6 weeks or so. Standing naked on the edge of the tub holding a denture cup full of vinegar up to the shower head in an attempt to unclog it makes you look totally ridiculous.

DO either check the stream coming out of the shower before undressing or at least lock your doors first. Your neighbors and/or grandchildren will thank you for this.

DON'T attempt to open a glass door while going through with your power chair by extending your leg and using your foot as a battering ram.

DO ask the hotel personnel to hold the door for you. Believe me, it really is quicker than opening it yourself and having to go to the emergency room to get your foot sewed back on.

DON'T wear a long, full, flowing dress while using your power chair. If you think it's humiliating to ask someone to open a door for you, try asking them to help you unwind your dress from your power train.

DO wear sensible clothing that is gorgeous, inexpensive, flattering, and makes you look like Cindy Crawford.. .oops...fell into a fantasy there, excuse me. Just wear something that doesn't get caught in your wheels, OK?

DON'T sneak up on people with your silent power chair. It's fun, I agree, to say something to someone who doesn't realize you are there and watch him clutch his heart and do that funny little break dance thing, but it is not always appreciated by the surprisee. Also, it could be dangerous if the person in question is holding a blunt object. Or a sharp object, for that matter.
DO hum softly to yourself or make some kind of noise to allow people to sense your presence, no, an air horn doesn't qualify, smarty pants.

I do hope these little nuggets of wisdom have been helpful to you. If you have any hints that you would like to pass along, please refrain from doing so. I'm pretty busy right now. I am putting ice on my swollen toe.

Keep an Attitude of Gratitude

This is the season to count our blessings. Sometimes it is difficult to think of how fortunate we really are when we are hurting, faced with difficulty in mobility, fighting with Durable Medical Equipment workers and the red tape that involves, but we really are very blessed.

"There is always someone worse off than you are." I have heard that a lot, but as I've told my friend Toni, if you have a broken leg, but the person next to you has Stage IV cancer, that does not mean your leg hurts you less. Your leg is still broken. You still deserve compassion.
What I'm trying to say is that if you remember all the things that you, personally, have been through and that you triumphed over these problems, you will realize that you are a winner. We are called survivors for a reason, yes?

My big problem is fatigue. Well, that and the fact that as a Type A personality, I never slow down. Oh yes, I know better, but life is so short and there are so many wonderful things out there. There is my family, all of whom live nearby, all of whom have birthdays, anniversaries, baptisms, weddings and yes, funerals. Then there are friends that I like to visit and places I like to go. I love to write, so I've volunteered to do an online polio newsletter, and the newsletter for my Cooperative, and my regular column here. I belong to a book club and a poetry club. My sister, whom I love dearly, needs me to drive her places since she no longer drives. So on the downside of this, I'm tired! I'm always tired. However, on the plus side, I will someday not be able to do all of this, so I enjoy it while I can.

Some of us really struggle financially, but there is Medicare/Medicaid to pay for our critical needs. I've seen films of polio survivors in third world countries who have absolutely no help to get wheelchairs or even crutches. I've seen polio survivors with thick calluses on their knees because they crawl wherever they go. What struck me the hardest while watching those films was that even though they had no help whatever, they were smiling. They were proud of their achievements, as well they should be, under these circumstances. They seemed grateful just to be alive.

My personal philosophy is that we should keep an attitude of gratitude for whatever blessings come our way. If you have food on your table, a roof over your head and at least one person who loves you (and there is no reason that person can't be you, yourself) you have reason to be grateful. Most of my friends are polio survivors and most of them have had many difficulties to overcome, but when we get together all of that is forgotten in our joy at seeing each other.

In this season of thankfulness, I have so much for which to be grateful. I am better off financially than I was when I was younger. My family lives close to me and I can see them whenever I like. I have a well maintained, comfortable, barrier free place to live. My neighbors here are, for the most part, very friendly and likeable. I have my little dog, who wakes me up every morning with kisses and is delighted to see me. There are children in my life. Nothing lifts the corners of my mouth more than children and dogs. And most of all, I have my readers. Those of you who follow my column make me feel as if I am contributing in a small way to making the corners of your mouths quirk upward now and then.

Happy Thanksgiving, everyone and Merry Christmas, Happy New Year, too!

EATING AN ELEPHANT

My closet is bulging at the seams. I look at the mess in there and get overwhelmed by all the stuff I've accumulated. When I moved here from Canada, I brought everything I owned because I wasn't sure where I'd be living. However, it all went into storage for the eight months it took me to find this apartment. Meanwhile, I replaced some (OK, a lot) of the clothing that was in the very back of the storage unit. I have gone through and donated some clothing from time to time. However, I keep replacing what I've discarded. I think it's a female thing.

Now, due to the fact that I don't walk much I have, well, sort of...shoot, I've gained weight, OK? So some of the stuff that escaped the last assault on the closet no longer fits me. I've replaced them but they are still there!

So now I need to get ruthless and donate a lot of unused used clothing. I can do that, I suppose. But the sheer enormity of the job is daunting. I can only stand for about 5 minutes before Mr. Sciatica and Mr. Bursitis come calling. Not much can be accomplished in 5 minutes, so I don't even start.

That's the wrong attitude. The voice in my head berates me for not even trying. You are familiar with that voice, I know you are. It's the polio dragon, taunting me. He's saying that I'm lazy and worthless and that asking for help is just not on the menu. "People don't want to stop their lives and do stuff for you!" So the problem continues to exist. Shoes that I've found don't work for me, but would work fine for someone else, blouses that are pretty, but don't fit me, countless pairs of pants...there they are, smirking in their assurance that they will never have to leave my comfy closet.

Which brings me to the title of this piece: Eating an Elephant. How do you eat an elephant? Simple, one small bite at a time. So tomorrow I will tackle the shoe problem. I have a box where I

can toss the shoes I no longer wear. Just that, no more. Once I get the box full, I can ask someone to take it to the place that accepts donated clothing. Or, I might even be able to put that box on my lap in my wheelchair and get it to the van on my own.
T
he next day, I can take everything off the shelf, just one shelf mind you, and sort that out. Or I could empty one drawer. Just one. It will take a long time to get it done and an able bodied person could surely do the entire thing in one day, but I'm not able bodied and frankly, I am not very fond of Mr. Sciatica or his brother Mr. Bursitis. They are, literally, a pain in the backside.

It might take me a month to eat that elephant, but the closet has been needing a cleaning for longer than that. Eventually, I will have a clean closet with no outgrown clothing or unwearable shoes. Won't it be nice? You never know, I just might develop a taste for elephant and use this theory on a few other huge projects that are lurking around here.

FAIR WARNING

For several years, I have wanted to attend the county fair held in nearby Denison. I have actually tried it a time or two, but found that my legs gave out long before I got to see all the exhibits. Last November, 1 got my Jazzy power chair, so this year when the fair opened I thought, "Hot dog! I am going to go see all the exhibits. I will see everything, from the needlework in the Women's Building to the Varied Industry building with its commercial booths. I might even have a Maid-Rite from the church's food booth!"

The Day arrived. I had five of my grandchildren and a neighbor child staying with me and they were restless. They wanted to do something. They whined. I scolded. We took a vote. Five of them wanted to go to the lake at the county park and swim. One of them did not. So we went to the lake, I dropped off the five who wanted to swim and took Cody, the odd man out, with me. We went to the fair!

I immediately noticed that the Fair Board had set aside some parking spots for handicapped parking! My grin split my face like a ripe coconut. This was great! Cody, being a helpful young man and as such fascinated with my Bruno Curbsider lift, unloaded my chair and off we went. Up the rather rough but still manageable graveled path we flew.

"I want to go in ALL the buildings," I told Cody. "Even the stuff I don't want to see, 1 want to see anyhow." We rolled up to the first building. Oooops. There was a concrete step about 3" high. My grin started to slip a bit. "Well, I really don't care much about the stuff in here, Cody," I lied. "Let's go on to the next one." Unfortunately, the same thing occurred at the second building. The third building another step..the bathrooms..more steps..the much anticipated Women's Building.. .not going in there, either, more steps. By this time, I was not such a happy camper.

We did manage to get into one building, nearly scraping the

undercarriage of my chair in the process. But could I actually go into the booths and look at the displays? Nope. Every booth was set on a concrete platform about 3" high. I couldn't sign up for door prizes, I couldn't look at the exhibits, I could not do anything. I was so disappointed. Luckily, I've been a Mom forever and a Granny almost that long, so I didn't cry in front of the K-I-D, but I was not far from it.

When we got back to our van, parked in the ridiculously useless handicapped parking spot, we found someone had maliciously keyed it, leaving a long, deep scratch down the side. Perfect. What a nice ending to a dreadful day.

Yes, I did complain to several Fair Board members. This is a small town, and I know them all personally. I then went back out to the lake and stopped at the Nature Center. Handicapped parking. OK. Wide enough doorway. Cautiously optimistic, I entered the building. FULL ACCESSIBILITY!! Yahoo! We looked at a tarantula, me from a distance, Cody up close. We viewed their boa constrictor, again, me from a distance, Cody up close. We admired and even petted the huge iguana, studied the fish in the aquarium, compared their Indian artifacts with the stone I'd found on my farm and which I am now even more convinced is a war club. I mentioned to the women working in this handicapped friendly place how much I appreciated the accessibility of this Nature Center and how disappointed I was in the fair. Surprise. They are members of the Fair Board, too.

At the end of the day, I had one scratched van, five sunburned and exhausted and (of course) starved young people, one helpful and pleased Cody, and one slightly mollified granny. Maybe next year, I can not only go TO the Fair, but be allowed inside.

GEESE

This morning I heard a lonely, honking sound. Looking up into the somewhat misty sky, I saw one lone goose flying north. He honked and honked but got no reply. It set me thinking about how similar we are to geese. Like geese, we humans mate for life. In actual practice this does not always work out but in theory at least, it is the goal. Like geese, we, too, need the support and companionship of others.

I thought about that goose all morning. Would he find the rest of the flock? Would he be strong enough to fly the vast distances all alone? Would he give up, stop flying after his friends die? This goose was all alone, it either had lost its mate or had not yet acquired one. There were no other geese to keep up with, no older or perhaps wiser geese to lead the way. Flying alone rather than in the traditional V formation meant that there were no leaders to break the wind, so this goose had a tougher job ahead of him than the others, those lucky enough to be in the flock. The others would take turns flying at the point of the V and bearing the force of the wind for the others. The other geese would also help each other by watching out for danger when they stopped to feed. Some of the geese in the flock would remain alert while others slept. My poor lonely goose would have to take his chances with hungry predators of all kinds, including man.

My support groups are my "flock. " Some of them have gone ahead of me down this path of Post Polio Syndrome and some are following behind me. The ones in the point have had it hardest, as they are the ones who got doctors to recognize that Post Polio Syndrome is a real disease. They showed that we are not, after a lifetime of being over achievers, suddenly lazy people who want to sit with our hands in our laps rather than be productive members of society.

We take care of each other, watch for "predators" that will shorten our lives or radically change our lifestyles. Predators like overuse of weakened polio muscles, depression, incorrect medications. We listen to each other's problems and share our own solutions and those we have heard from other sources. When one of us benefits, we share our good fortune, in much the same way as one of the flock will share a feeding place with the rest. We watch out for each other and welcome each other to rest with us on this journey of ours. We have a common goal and common problems and we try to take our turns at breasting the wind for our fellow travelers.

If you feel as if you are a lonely goose, honking into the empty sky, please find a support group near you, share your problems and accept the friendship and compassion of your fellow travelers. I hope that goose finally caught up with the rest of his family, too.

GIVING IN

So often I hear my fellow polio survivors say, "I refuse to give in." That usually means that they refuse to use the adaptive aids that are so necessary to their continued independence, "I'll never use a wheelchair, not till I cannot walk a single step. What will my neighbors say if they see me using a walker/cane?"

I was thinking about that today as my dog and I were out for our morning stroll. She walks, I roll. Robert E. Lee came to mind. Don t ask me why. My mind, early in the morning, tends to roam around untethered, leaping from idea to idea like an antelope on speed.

Robert E. Lee, by all accounts an honorable and proud man, nevertheless had to give in. At some point in that awful war, he realized that to continue would cost more than it was worth. He cut his losses and gave in as graciously as he could. He could not justify the losses, knowing that the end result would not be victory.

We could think of it that way, too. Our little motor neuron soldiers are dying. To stubbornly refuse to allow them rest is similar to continuing a winless war, no matter the cost. Perhaps this struggle is seen in a romantic light. Perhaps we think it is nobler to fight on to the bitter end, never letting up, even knowing that we will be defeated in the end. We may have a picture of ourselves going out in a blaze of glory, a hero to the end.

Reality is somewhat different, I'm afraid. There is no glory in fighting to the bitter end. There is ignominious defeat or there is honorable surrender. Post polio will win. It had a head start, after all, in the blitzkrieg that wiped out half our motor neurons or more in the opening sally of the conflict. Continuing to battle will only deplete our forces, leaving us with nothing as we leave the field.

There is a victory of sorts. We can call in help from canes, walkers, wheelchairs, whatever is available to us. We can leave the field bloody but unbowed. We can save our remaining battalions for other pursuits. We are still heroes. We fought the good fight. Now we can put our wounded soldiers to good use as we retire from combat. Retirement is not so bad. Now we can rest, enjoy our retirement from the battle, become civilians, wearing our battle scars proudly. There is no shame in giving in. Like old soldiers, we recognize each other and form a bond that others will never know.

Has Anyone Seen My Dignity?

Apparently, your memory is not the first thing to go as the Golden
Years stalk you relentlessly. It's your dignity. Yep, the stuff that
hasn't dried up or just quit working at all leaks or creaks or starts
to develop a faint odor, which may or may not remain faint.
Aging still beats the alternative, but some days it is a photo finish.

I am, as you know, a "woman of a certain age," just which age is
frankly none of your business. I try to dress nicely and aim for
elegance. OK, I said I aimed for it, I did not say I hit the bullseye.
I can still walk, but dignity is definitely not part of that scene.
Not when I tend to list heavily to port and lurch into unsuspecting
door frames and unwary people. I'm much more graceful in my
power chair, barring the odd toe that may get crushed when I'm in
a hurry. Not my fault that my chair has such a wimpy little horn
that goes beep beep when, to be affective, it should go BEEP
BEEP. So there is that. Then there is the fact that my thigh
muscles are pretty much useless. Not even good for decorative
purposes. No, I look like I'm ready to play an invisible cello as I
sit there, knees spraddled. Not elegant, not even close.

Trying to be considerate of others, I stay out of crowded places
where other people may not want to become mangled as I wend
my merry way through the room. I attended a meal in the
building next door last Saturday. There is a woman here in town,
Myong Vanteicher, who is the best cook I know. She provides a
Chinese buffet once a month there and then a week later, the same
thing here in my building. She charges only enough to pay for
the ingredients. The problem is that while the dining area here in
my building is spacious and very easy to get around in, the one
next door is cramped and next to impossible to maneuver my
chair between the closely spaced tables. I could skip that meal, I
suppose. Are you crazy or do you just think I am?? Pass up
Myong's tempura shrimp? I don't think so!

I solved the problem, I thought, by simply parking my chair in the back of the room and walking through the buffet line. It worked great, too, till I stepped on something while carrying my loaded plate back to the table. Yep, I did a little impromptu break dancing there, complete with air born shrimp, fried rice in my hair and down the front of that day's attempt at elegant attire. My skirt, which had a slit in the back originally, ended up mostly two flaps of cloth with my very inelegant lower extremities flapping in the breeze.

Everyone rushed to help me get up. I'm not sure exactly how I managed to land on what I laughingly call my Good knee, the one I always land on and that has fluid on it as a result, but of course no good break dance would be complete without it. I managed to waddle back to my chair, red faced and minus the delicious shrimp for which I'd attended the buffet in the first place. Somehow I did get another serving of food, and I laughed about providing the entertainment for the day. One woman said she'd missed it. I told her I was not doing an encore and "You snooze, you lose."

Old age, as the saying goes, is not for sissies. Dignity, elegance, graceful mobility are all pretty much a pipe dream at this stage of my life, but do I really care? I mean, do I mind so much that I'd avoid going to that Chinese buffet? Not on your life. I really believe in the saying that if you can laugh at yourself, you will have an endless supply of entertainment. If you can't, I'll be happy to laugh at you for free. You are welcome!

Hello

Listen up, Brain. We body parts have had a discussion and we want to bring a few things to your attention. You don't know everything, you know. As Left Leg of this conglomeration, I would appreciate it if you would keep from insinuating that I'm worthless. If I weren't here, even damaged as I am, you would topple over. The polio virus did a number on me, I admit that. And, OK, I'm not pretty. I won't lie, I know that I 'm skinnier than Right Leg, but look how hard I've tried to be everything you want in a leg. It is not my fault that I was left with so few motor neurons that I can barely function.

And I'm Right Leg. I've been hauling this whole body around since we were four years old. I'm doing pretty good, I think. I believe a few less Twinkies and Pepsi might be helpful. I'm not Super Leg, you know!

This is Back, here. There are times when I realize I'm giving you more grief than you can handle. Sorry about that. You have to realize that with Left Leg being less useful...hold on, Left Leg, I did not say useless! I just mean that with your not being your old self (there, is that better?) there's a bit of a twist on me and I can't help complaining about it. I agree about the Twinkies, by the way.

Right Arm speaking. Sorry about dropping your grandmother's crystal bowl the other day. I did help you sweep it up. However, we need to talk about those crutches. I'm just not meant to do the work that Legs were designed for. Left Arm and our Hands have just about had it. It's no wonder we are losing our grip! We think you should at least try to have a little consideration for us. Polio zapped us, too. Not as bad as Legs, but still, we also lost a lot of neurons and we've worked very hard to help you get places and do things.

This is your Right Hip talking. With the difference in length between Right Leg and Left Leg and the slight twist in Back, life is not wonderful for me and Left Hip. Sometimes the scoliosis twists us till we are almost dizzy. We would definitely vote for fewer Twinkies, too.

So, as spokespart, for this body, I, Left Leg, have some suggestions. One is to try really hard to eat healthier. Come on, it's hard enough to drag you around without your gaining even more weight. Another suggestion is that you show a little appreciation for us. We've worked really hard for you for a very long time, under conditions that would make a lesser body give up the ghost. It hurts our feelings when you stand in front of the mirror and disparage us.

"Oh, look how crooked I stand. I list to port and I fall so easily."

You complain that we aren't pretty. Well, excuse me, but it wasn't our fault, really that you look like this. Blame it on Polio, he's the Bad Guy. He tried to kill you, but we didn't let him. He tried to make your life sad and lonely, but we didn't let that happen.

OK, lecture over. You can go back to what you were doing. No, not that exercise bike! Don't you ever listen? Conserve to Preserve. Pace. Give it up, Spanky, you are never going to be an athlete, but you can have a good life anyhow. Most athletes abuse their bodies even more than you do, and many of them have to retire at an early age from working too hard. What's that you say, Brain? You couldn't live without us? Darn right and don't you forget it!

Holidaze

By the time you read this, Thanksgiving will be looming large and then comes The Big C...no, not Cancer, Christmas! Shopping, crowds, overeating, gaining weight, all the usual holiday activities. It's difficult for polio survivors to deal with some of this.

Personally, I shop online as much as I can. I usually keep a "stash box" with gift items in it. I shop all year round, looking for bargains or for items I think will please someone on my Christmas list. Actual shopping, as in a store, is something I do not enjoy. I enjoy it least on Black Friday or Boxing Day, the day after Christmas.

People lose their minds on those two days. A woman who is a sensible, kind hearted, compassionate person the rest of the year, may turn into a wild eyed maniac composed mostly of elbows, knees and gimlet-eyed glares. Do not, and I cannot stress this enough, do NOT get between this woman and the bargain she has her heart set on. She will clamber right over you, standing on your lap if need be, to get to The Bargain. Thankfully, this type of woman, your Serious Shopper, does not wear stiletto heeled shoes. No, she will wear comfortable walking shoes because she plans to be on her feet till the stores all close and the night watchman drags her to the sidewalk, armed with a gun and a drooling Doberman Pinscher. Those stilettos could puncture an artery if she is forced to climb over you. The walking shoes will merely leave bruises.

Take my advice and stay home on Black Friday unless your power chair has caterpillar tracks to bulldoze your way through a crowd, and armor plating would be advisable, too. A helmet, goggles, and a stainless steel jump suit would be suitable Black Friday Shopping Wear. Boxing Day, December 26, is not quite as dangerous, but can also be very unpleasant if you have a low tolerance for anger, disappointment, and grumpy sales people. You can't blame the sales staff for being cranky. The same item

Mrs. Super Shopper nearly killed people to reach on Black Friday often turns out to be not what was wanted after all. So back she goes on Boxing Day to return it in the bashed in box that was thrown at her by the ungrateful child/husband she was trying so hard to please.

Overeating is the holiday sport I do enjoy All those Thanksgiving pies, the stuffing, the turkey (which is not that highly caloric if you eat a human sized portion, but where's the joy in that?) Mashed potatoes, cranberry relish, cornbread stuffing...very hard to resist. I have one thing going for me: I don't care much for pumpkin and there is an unbreakable rule that any treat made in the month of November must, by law, contain pumpkin. Pumpkin lattes, anyone? So all I have to do is remind myself that whatever tempting looking treat is giving me the come-hither look, it likely has pumpkin in it. In December, I can avoid almost all chocolate baked goods because the December unbreakable rule is that all chocolate must be accompanied by peanut butter. I hate peanut butter. I do have a hard time trying to convince myself that pecan pie or cornbread stuffing have either pumpkin or peanut butter in them.

And of course, the Number One Holiday Pastime is...drumroll, please...gaining weight! In all modesty, I must admit that I am a heavy weight Champion in that division. I will try, truly I will, to substitute celery for cornbread, lettuce for pecan pie, and sugar free carob cookies for mashed potatoes. Really. Honest, would I lie? By the way, I have a nice section of ocean front property in Iowa for sale, if you are interested.

HOW TO TAME YOUR DRAGON

Have you heard the saying, "The best way to defeat an enemy is
to make him your friend"? That, I think, is the approach we need
to take with the polio dragon. "If you can't beat them, join them"
is another useful motto. I know for a fact, that we are never going
to beat the polio dragon. He won in the very first round. How,
then, do we deal with him?

There are several ways of handling the polio dragon. You can use
every motor neuron he left you to keep him at bay. You can drag
yourself around on crutches, exhausted and in pain, in order not to
let the dragon win by putting you in The Dreaded Wheelchair. Or
you can lurch along without the crutches, without your brace or
braces, bumping into walls and furniture and, in your own mind,
not looking as though you are handicapped. To other people, you
probably look like a drunk or like someone who is severely
handicapped and in denial. It causes them to pity you. I don't
mind compassion, but I hate pity. This method is not very
effective.

Another way is the way karate students are taught. Use your
opponents attack as your defense. In other words, roll with the
punches. This keeps your opponent off balance. Instead of
fighting to stay out of The Dreaded Wheelchair, embrace it as a
friend. You might discover that it really isn't The Dreaded
Wheelchair, but the Blessed Wheelchair. Oh, there will be times,
when you are out and about and forgot to charge The Blessed
Wheelchair and you will bless it and yourself in a loud voice. All
blessings are a bit mixed, after all.

This is not to say the polio dragon will be defeated. No, sad to
say, that won't happen. It might make his swipes at you less
effective, though. He destroyed so many neurons right at the
outset of the battle that you have a very sadly depleted armory
and no way to buy more. His goal now is to make you, yourself,
destroy the rest of your weapons. Every time you exhaust
yourself in fighting this dreaded foe, you use up more of your

resources. Every time you use an assistive device, you conserve a bit of your dwindling supply. It only makes sense to go into a siege mind set. Hoard your weapons, saving them only for defense.

This dragon would like nothing better than to see you totally defeated, all motor neurons burnt to a crisp, not one muscle left in useable condition. If you want to at least stop his damage, you have to fight smarter, not harder. Take a nap when you need one. Say NO to activities that require you to do things that are exhausting or too difficult. Wear a smile as armor against those who don't understand that when you say you can't do something, it means you cannot, not that you will not. Be firm, but pleasant. Don't try to deny that the dragon has damaged you, but don't let him do further harm.

Eventually, you and the dragon can sign a peace treaty. If you don't continue to fight him, he won't have occasion to strike out at you. Maybe you can even reach a point where you use his fiery breath to roast hot dogs and marshmallows.

INSPIRATION PORN

The other day, on Facebook, I saw a video of a woman in a wheelchair giving a speech to an audience of mostly non-disabled people. She said she lived a normal life, like everyone else, but that a charitable group approached her, wanting to give her some kind of achievement award. "For what?" she wanted to know. "I haven't done anything!" When they told her she was being given the award for just doing what everyone else was doing but from a wheelchair, she got a bit incensed.

This is the part that is hard to explain. She did not want to be an inspiration. She feels that this attitude toward people with disabilities objectifies them. I agree. Anyone who regularly reads my column knows how I feel about labels, about being 'cute' and about pigeonholes. I just didn't know how to express it as well as she did. She calls this kind of thing "Inspiration Porn."

People have asked me how I can remain so cheerful. I know they mean well, but exactly why should I not be cheerful? I use a power chair instead of walking, but many of them play golf using a golf cart instead of walking. My life is good. It would not necessarily be better if I'd not had polio. In fact, although polio can be and often is a pain in the neck and points south of there, it is through my association with polio survivors that I have become a writer, have done the traveling I so loved, met people who are now my family of the heart.

I don't know about you, but I have no desire to be a poster child for Don't Let This Happen To You. I don't want people to look at me and think, "Oh, poor thing. She's so brave." True, I have had moments of bravery, but they had nothing to do with my having had polio. I think it was pretty brave of Carolann and me to travel as we did, camping in the van, cooking at rest areas, seeing so much of both our countries and meeting so many online friends in person. That would be a brave thing to do for anyone, don't you think? Okay, maybe foolhardy is a better description, but still...It might be considered brave of me to get up in front of a group of people and speak. It is said that most people are more afraid of public speaking than of death. That is "most people," not just people with a disability or able bodied people. Again, nothing to do with my wheelchair.

There are challenges in life for everyone, with or without a disability. In fact, when you look at the word "disability," it simply means an inability to do something. I'm here to tell you, everyone has an inability to do something. Some people cannot sing, some can't dance, some cannot spell, some people cannot even read. These same people, however, can do many other things. I think I speak for most of us when I say that I do not want to be an inspiration.

There was a cute meme on Facebook today. It said, "Do not follow in my footsteps. I walk into walls."

INVISIBILITY AND THE FURNITURE GIRL

Are you aware that there is a quick and easy, although not inexpensive, method to become invisible? There is. Sit in a wheelchair. I'd never have believed this had I not checked it out personally in my Jazzy.

I don't always use that power chair as I can still walk and if the distance is no more than a few feet, it is sometimes easier to walk it than to unload the Jazzy from the back of my van. However, I do use the wheelchair when I shop and when I go to church.

Now this power chair of mine weighs a fair amount and it is bright blue. Add to that the fact that it is carrying a not insubstantial passenger. Doesn' t sound like it would be invisible, does it? But yes, it is and I am, when I am in it.

Last weekend I attended a brunch at a local restaurant, a breakfast buffet. In spite of the noise of the chairs and tables I rearranged as I bulled my way over to the line, a woman calmly walked around me and got in line ahead of me. To her, I was invisible and also not a person. I was Furniture Girl, an article in her way, so she stepped around me as she would an errant card table. Only when I nudged her ever so gently with my Jazzy did she turn around. Then she looked right through me and continued to fill her plate. I had achieved invisibility! Since then, I've noticed this same phenomenon in Wal Mart and the grocery store. I will be reaching over to get a carton of milk and someone will get in front of me, put his/her elbow firmly in my face and get their own dairy products. I would put this down to rudeness, but I have never had this happen when I am not in the chair. Not once. So I assume this is due to my newly acquired invisibility.

Surely there must be a good use for this new talent. I couldn't use it to rob a bank. As a farmer who is deeply and probably permanently in debt, I sort of feel I've already robbed that bank. My basic honesty and muscular conscience (the only muscle I have that I can rely on is that darn conscience) preclude using it for any type of wrong-doing. So to what good use could I put it? I will have to think about this one.

Why didn't those of you already in wheelchairs let me in on this? And, by the way, it doesn't work on children. They see more with their hearts than their eyes, so I am still clearly visible to them. I know, because as I was trying to get my groceries, I pulled up next to a shopping cart with a little girl in it. Our eyes were on a level and she immediately began a conversation with me. "Hi!" she twinkled. "Hi, yourself, " I answered. Such witty repartee. It put a big, although undoubtedly invisible, smile on my face as I hummed my way through the rest of the shopping, casually running over a toe here and there just to see the startled look on people's faces as they wondered what was happening to the ends of their shoes.

It Depends

This probably applies a lot more to the women in our group, but you never know. The subject is Depends...adult diapers,incontinence briefs, call them what you will. At some point in life, these things could become something we, well, Depend on.

A dear friend of mine called me the other night and said that she had had a little problem that cropped up on a trip she was taking with her husband and some friends. As my friend went to the bathroom, she noticed she was bleeding rectally, no doubt due to a pain medication she was taking. She was forced to get the adult diapers till the problem was resolved.

My friend is a beautiful woman, classy and elegant. She buys lingerie, not just undergarments, the good stuff. The lacy stuff. The Fantasy Stuff. Depends really don't fit that category. She admits they are comfortable, much more so than she had at first expected. They don't crinkle or make plastic-y sounds when she moves. But they are very utilitarian in appearance. Very Depend-able, if you will.

She explained that she immediately thought of me when she realized this issue needed to be addressed. Yes, my friends think of me when there are incontinence problems. Some people remind their friends of beautiful things, roses, moonlight, stuff like that. My friends think of me and adult diapers. At least they think of me, right? I choose to believe this is because I make them laugh so hard tears run down their legs.

Anyway, the problem as my friend sees it, is that the diapers are just not pretty. If we all write to the company that makes these items, and say how we'd like a bit more bling for our buck, would it help? Gail suggested a kit you could buy, a sort of after market add on, that contained some sequins or rhinestones or maybe a stencil and a magic marker so you could draw a lacy pattern on them.

If I get enough responses to warrant the travel, I might be convinced to go to the factory and lead a protest. We could "march"around in our wheelchairs with big signs stuck in our crutch holders. Let's see, what could we put on the signs?

SEQUINS FOR OUR SOAKERS! Perhaps? Or maybe DEPENDS ARE DRAB! Who is with me? Anyone want to go picket a factory? I have room for four people and one wheelchair in my van, but a walker will also fit on the lift with the wheelchair. If you wouldn't mind holding the parts on your laps in the back seat, we could probably accommodate a travel scooter that comes apart, too.

While this project might not, at first glance,seem very appealing to our male members, I would like to point out that a happy spouse is always a good thing. If you happen to be married to a disgruntled female Depends wearer, it might be in your best interests to go along with this business. If you don't want to march with us, I'll gladly provide paint and brushes so you can paint some signs for us. Remember, if Momma aint happy, aint nobody happy.

Lessons Learned

My Jazzy 1105 power chair was delivered on Thursday. I have entertained myself since then, learning how to run the darn thing. Here are some hints you might find useful in case you are ever "sent to the electric chair."

1. If you are right handed, do not put the joystick on the right side. A friend of mine gently reminded me that if you are running the chair with your right hand, you are going to have to carry things, open doors and generally do everything with your left hand. So put the joystick on the opposite side from your dominant hand.

2. 2. Since Jazzys do not have keys, disengage the little doohickeys under the chair that engage the motor if you are going to leave the chair unattended while children are in your home. It's easily reversed when you want to use the chair. Under no circumstances let the kids see how this is done. They will figure it out sooner or later, but meanwhile, you can keep some of your plaster on your walls. Also, if you have parked the chair outside the bathroom door, it will still be there when you are ready to get back into it.

3. If your pet is slower on the uptake than mine is, carry a squirt bottle with you and squirt the pet who is lying trustingly in your path instead of making him into carpet kill, the indoor equivalent of roadkill. In the case of my cat, there is no problem. As soon as she saw this chair, Kelli knew what she was in for and she heads for higher ground before I even get the chair turned on. However, some pets are not as bright or are more trusting of their humans. Not to even mention the discomfort to the cat/dog, it is rather bad for the chair to run over animals with it. The same applies, of course, for young children. It also really upsets their parents.

4. If you find yourself with the arm-rests of the Jazzy wedged under the armrests of the couch and panic, you can push the couch into the middle of the room. I decline

to say exactly how I gained this nugget of wisdom. Just trust me. It can be done.

5. There are medical hinges available for doorways that are just a tad too narrow for the chair. These hinges allow the door to open flat against the wall instead of sticking out at the hinges. Alternatively, you can widen the doorway yourself by repeatedly hitting it with the Jazzy till enough chunks fall off to allow easy access. The beauty of this method is that the holes in the door will coincide exactly with the shape of the chair. I intended to use the "medical hinges" option, but unfortunately while waiting to order them, I have already used option number 2.

I hope this is helpful to all of you. Perhaps in my next column I can give you some hints on using a lift for a van.

Mourning Glories

Grief comes in stages: Denial, Anger, Bargaining, Depression and finally Acceptance. As I've told friends who've lost loved ones, we all go through these stages and it takes as long as it takes. We polio survivors also grieve for our lost abilities, and in much the same way.

When I first started to suffer from PPS, I was in denial. Nonsense, polio happened eons ago when I was a child. I'm fine now. Of course, I fell a lot and I always had a bruise coming or going. That was because I was a klutz who tripped over her own shadow. I was told that I needed to go back into a brace. WHAT??? No, I don't think so!

Finally, the fact that my ankle turned over so often that a callous formed and then split convinced me that maybe I should get a brace. I was not happy about this. I had gone through surgeries so that I would never have to wear a brace again. How dare they say I needed this! How dare this even happen to me! I'd worked so hard with the dreaded Physical Terrorists, did the painful exercises religiously, went dancing, skating, swimming, all to conquer polio.

I had reached the Bargaining stage by this time: I'll wear the stupid brace if you insist, but only when I have to walk on rough ground. It's ugly and it doesn't fit in my shoe. In fact, it is attached to a pair of those ugly shoes I swore I'd never set foot in again. I want to wear pretty shoes, like other women!

After wearing the brace awhile, I discovered that the callous on my polio affected foot no longer split and filled my shoe with blood. I'd long ago learned to ignore that pain, so I was surprised at finding it gone. I wasn't falling so often, either. I still lurched into doorways but not as often. That was good, but those shoes. Oh, those ugly, ugly shoes. I felt like an old woman, no longer young and fashionable. I would never wear dresses or shorts again, because then people could see the Hated Brace. I was almost sick at heart. I'd really tried so hard to overcome my disability and darn it, here it was, back again. This time in so visible a form that there was no hiding it.

Gradually, I accepted the brace as the tool it was meant to be. I could walk across the field to bring my husband his lunch when he was working there. While doing chores, I could carry the milk into the separator room without spilling it. I found nice looking dress pants to wear when I dressed up. Gradually, I even grew brave enough to wear dresses and shorts again. Summer in Iowa is a great motivator for wearing something cooler!

Then it happened. Hurrying around to get dinner ready by the time my husband came in from the field, I stepped on something on the floor. Down I went, my body twisting over the Hated Brace. I got a spiral fracture in my polio affected leg. Rats. Back to square one in the Grieving Game.

This could not be happening! Oh, no, that leg won't bear weight. I'm back to crutches, and a manual chair. It took 18 months for that leg to heal enough that I could walk on it. Meanwhile, I'd lost what little muscle tone I had and could no longer lift the leather and steel brace I'd finally accepted. I had to find a brace light enough for me to be able to lift my foot, yet strong enough to keep me from falling.

Weeks, months, and years went by while I struggled to stay out of the power chair that was looming large. On one memorable visit to my polio doctor, I got a real slap upside my head. A rude awakening, if you will. I found I absolutely could not walk from one end of the hospital where my doctor was to the opposite corner where my orthotist worked. I claimed one of the hospital's manual chairs and got another good Wallop of Wisdom. I couldn't push myself in that chair! You know I tried, I am a card carrying polio survivor and we always try. I managed somehow. When I finally got back in my car for the drive home, two hours away, my head was buzzing with fatigue.

I knew I'd have to give in and get a power chair. My doctor had no problem prescribing one for me and a friend of mine ran the Durable Medical Equipment place in town, so very soon I had a power chair.

Would you believe I had to go, again, to the beginning of the grieving process? The chair sat there. I refused to use it. My friend, the one who'd sold it to me, asked why I wasn't using it. I told her it made my back hurt. She looked at me with that look your Mom gives you when you try to tell her a story. She whipped out her tools, adjusted the back of the chair and told me to plop my behind in it and not to be so stubborn.

It's too late to make a long story short, but I did finally accept the chair, got a ramp installed on my house, put a lift in my van, and discovered freedom. I could now go to the post office or the store without pain and exhaustion. What a concept! I could go to the zoo! I've always lived within driving distance of the Henry Doorly Zoo in Omaha, but I'd never been there. I discovered a whole new world of things I could do now that I had wheels.

I've moved since those days and I've replaced that chair a couple of times. I now live in an accessible building and can take my power chair to the park, to the grocery store, to the library, to my dog's vet, to the movie theater...and if I want to roam farther, I can load it in my van and go some more. Once I moved through all the stages of grieving for my lost abilities, I found that life is really good. It just takes as long as it takes.

Of Sandals and Street Fairs

Summer is over, but this is the best time of year for a street fair here in Iowa. September and October are beautiful with cool mornings and evenings and warm temperatures during midday. However, I must warn those Able Bodied Persons who attend these street fairs. I will attend any and all accessible activities in my area.

The streets may be blocked off to vehicular traffic, but my wheelchair will still be able to toodle all over the place. Therefore, do not wear sandals to a street fair in Denison, Iowa. There may be other places that also should be off limits to anything but steel toed work boots, but definitely take heed if you are going to be in Denison.

While maneuvering my way through the crowds in an attempt to enter the supermarket, I inadvertently, really, I swear it was totally by accident, ran over a man's foot. In my defense, I completely forgot that my 180 lb. power chair, with it's bright red and yellow seat cover, and containing my own not insubstantial and also gaudily clothed body, was invisible. I did not allow for that fact when the nice couple offered to make a path for me through the crowd.

How was the sandal-wearing person to know that they were making the path for an invisible, though brightly colored wheelchair? So, of course, he barged right in front of me, sticking his stocking clad, sandal shod toesies right under my wheels. To our mutual chagrin, even invisible wheelchairs are quite heavy. It seems that pain renders invisibility null and void. As he was howling in pain, he looked right at me and said, "Hey! You ran over my foot!"

I apologized several times as he hopped up and down, holding his injured foot, but he appeared to remain unmollified. Had he been wearing the recommended steel toed work boots, he would not even have noticed, but sadly that was not the case. Perhaps, once his toenail grows back, he might consider wearing those boots.

I've thought about getting an air horn to help me weave my way through crowds, but someone once told me that an unexpected air horn coming from an invisible power chair could cause a heart attack. I wouldn't want that! Running over an entire prostrate person might tip my invisible chair over! Then where would we be? I am visualizing a herd of people trying to climb over a heap containing an invisible chair, an invisible woman, and possibly a very visible sandal-wearing man. Probably not, though. I'm pretty sure that I did enough damage that Mr. Sandal Man could be driving his own invisible chair for awhile. So sorry.

One 'Flu Over

This has been a very bad winter for the 'flu. Or maybe it's been a great year for the 'flu but much less wonderful for its victims. One couple in my building spent weeks in the hospital and in rehab after contracting the Real 'Flu...Influenza A. We were all told that if we started coughing or ran a fever or had any of the other 'flu-like systems, to see a doctor. My brother's girlfriend mentioned during a phone call that Jerry had been coughing all night. I insisted he go right to the doctor and be checked. It was not at my suggestion that the doctor did a nasal swab on him. I want that perfectly clear...not my idea at all.

I, of course, never get sick so I assumed, as I usually do, that the rules were meant for the rest of you. Not for me. I never get sick, remember?

Fast forward to Sunday morning, January 25. I coughed myself awake and looked around for the freight train that had obviously run over me, backed up and did it again. My head was pounding, someone had taken all my bones out and rapped them on some cement till they were misshapen and reinserted them in the wrong spots. While they were at it, they sandpapered my eyeballs to a glossy sheen. I staggered to the bathroom and found some Aleve, took two and went back to bed. This exercise repeated itself on Monday, Tuesday, and Wednesday. By Wednesday afternoon, I could be up for short periods, but my legs were very wobbly. (I know, at my age, everything is pretty wobbly, be nice to me, I'm sick.) By Thursday, I could be up, but I was either freezing or sweating. Sometimes both at the same time. Every small effort brought forth buckets of sweat.

Knowing I couldn't do anything requiring much effort, I decided to start working on the forthcoming issue of Polio Perspective. When just sitting in my chair thinking caused perspiration to sluice off my face and hair, forming a small lagoon under my desk, I decided maybe I should go to the doctor. My son Jim took my keys, loaded my chair and my sweaty, clammy self into the van and we were off.

I may as well confess right now that I lied to my doctor's nurse. Yes, I did, mea culpa. I came into the office in my power chair because my son Jim is wonderful but expecting him to carry me would be asking too much. So, the nurse, seeing the power chair, assumed I could not walk. She led me past the scales, only hesitating a minute while asking if I thought I could stand long enough to get weighed. I probably could have, but this looked like a great opportunity to skip that part of the torture, so I said No. With a straight face. My doctor and I have already hashed the weight thing out. The first time I ever saw him, I started out by saying that I know I'm overweight but that as a polio survivor, exercise was not exactly recommended, so let's just work on the stuff that can be fixed. We reached an understanding that I'd never had with a doctor before.

The sweet little nurse took my blood pressure which was surprisingly lower than normal for me and left the room. My doctor came in, checked my ears, my throat, listened to my lungs and said that he could do a nasal swab but didn't think it was necessary. (Ha ha, Jerry. Also neener neener.) The doctor said I probably didn't have that serious Influenza A, but I did have Parainfluenza. My understanding is that this form of 'flu is sort of the knockoff WalMart version of the real 'flu. Very fitting for this woman who always shops the clearance racks. Oh, I didn't feel I'd been cheated by getting this cheaper version of the illness. It didn't have all the bells and whistles of Influenza A, lacking the high fever component as well as the pneumonia attachment, but it had lots of coughing, sneezing, wobbliness...all your main features without which it would not dare to call itself even a knockoff type 'flu.

I was also told that even though I'd already been sick for most of a week, I still had at least a week of this nonsense left. Tylenol, rest, lots of fluids. Thank goodness for Meals on Wheels so I get at least one good well balanced meal a day.

If only this 'flu caused weight loss. Wouldn't that be great? But no, that never happens for me. But it is a great excuse to pamper myself, loll around in my jammies, have the grandkids wait on me a little bit. Life could be worse. Meanwhile, I hope the rest of you stay well. If you feel you must have the 'flu, I'd say go for the kind I got. You don't need all the attachments that come with Influenza A. Trust me.

POLIO DRAGON TO BE EVICTED

Dateline Dow City, IA... In a rare interview with Polio Dragon this week, Millie Lill made some startling discoveries.

Millie: Good morning, Mr. Dragon.

Polio Dragon: Good morning, Mrs. Lill.

Millie: Are you THE Polio Dragon, the one we hear so much about?

Polio Dragon: Well, not really. Actually, I'm one of several Dragons. We have a pretty large extended family.

Millie: Really?

Polio Dragon: Yes, I'm just the small Dragon you swallowed awhile back. My job is just to shoot flames out your throat from time to time to remind you not to eat anything that tastes good.

Millie: But there are others?

Polio Dragon: Oh, my, yes. There is the large Dragon who lives in your legs and sends those lovely middle of the night cramps, and our brother who lives in your back and makes it spasm. One of our sisters loves to coil up around your head and try to split it open. She has almost succeeded in some of your peers.

Millie: I hate to be rude here, but why on earth do you do those horrible things to us?

Polio Dragon: Because we can, Ma'am, because we can.

Millie: Surely there is a way to prevent this torture.

Polio Dragon: Oh, yes, there is. And I'm so sure you won't do it, that I'm going to tell you what it is.

Millie: Tell me!

Polio Dragon: Well...it's called Rest.

Millie: Hmm. That's pretty simple, can it be that easy?

Polio Dragon: You call this easy? How long have you been a polio survivor anyway? Tell me this, Mrs. Lill: how many naps have you had this week?

Millie: Uhhh.. .well.. .I keep meaning to lie down in the afternoon, but I have so much to do. I hate to waste the time sleeping when I have other j obs that need to be completed. My grandkids are growing up fast and I need to spend time with them, and there is my sister...she needs me from time to time...

Polio Dragon: See? Didn't I tell you?

Millie: I may not be able to get rid of all of you Dragons, but I do have a plan to get rid of YOU.

Polio Dragon: Oh, yeah?

Millie: Yeah! I'm going to have that pesky hiatal hernia fixed and you won't have a place to live anymore. So there!

Polio Dragon: How will you know not to eat tasty foods? Who is going to warn you about the dangers of eating at bedtime?

Millie: I'll manage, somehow.

Polio Dragon: (aside) Now let's see if she figures out how to evict the other Dragons by getting some rest every day. Betcha my brothers will still have a place to live for a long while!

POLIO WORD SEARCH

If you are expecting a grid to appear and a list of words, I am
truly sorry. The polio word search is a totally different game. A
polio survivor can be rattling along (chatterboxitis is a well
known polio residual) when all of a sudden...what was the word I
was going to use? This leads to a fun game played by all polio
survivors. Sometimes we play via email, sometimes in person.
Polio Survivor 1: ...and then I saw this really
remarkable....ummmm, you know, that thing. I think it starts with
an r. Maybe not. Polio Survivor 2: Is it bigger than a....oh,
shoot...you know, you keep that sliced stuff in it so it won't get all
dried out? PS1: Breadbox? Is what bigger than a breadbox? PS2:
The really remarkable thing you saw...remember? Is it bigger
than a breadbox? PS1: I have no idea, I can't even remember what
it was I saw now.

This scenario is played out over and over. PS1 will, in all
likelihood wake up at 3 am shouting "Rifle! It was a rifle!" At
which point his/her spouse will jump out of bed and have 911
dialed before PS1 can explain that it was a lost word that just
found its way home.

I talk to many polio survivors via the internet every day. None of
us can remember anything. I am thinking of inventing one of
those, you know...they suck stuff up...no, not a straw...a vacuum,
yes that's the word. What was I saying? Oh, yes, I am thinking
of inventing a vacuum that will suck up all the words we lose in
our everyday conversations and restore them to our heads where
they belong.

I can see it now...a group of polio survivors are sitting around a
table, each holding some playing cards in his hands. No one can
remember if they were playing Hearts or Euchre, so they lapse
into a conversation instead. One woman is telling her friend
about a new place to shop, the men are swapping fishing stories.
The conversation is peppered with "Oh, you know what I mean"
and "I'll think of it in a minute, just hang on." Words are
wandering off, some of them not just leaving but taking hostages
as well.

TADA! In I come with my new invention, the thingie...you know what I mean. I plug it in and start vacuuming up the words that have drifted into a pile in the corner of the kitchen. Then I get a large box and dump the bag.

"Hey! Who was talking about fishing? I found "flycasting" in here. Did someone say something about hot flashes? This word is sort of bent and scuffed, but I think it's "menopause." Anybody need a perfectly good "repercussions?" Ooooooooops. I think I have to adjust the settings here...all that is left is a pile of odd vowels, four exclamation marks and several hundred commas. Wait, maybe those aren't all commas. They could be semi colons....maybe this one is an apostrophe. Anyone want any of these before I dump them in the wastebasket?"

I'm thinking of perhaps opening a used word store. I could vacuum up all those lost words, dust them off, polish them up a bit and sort them alphabetically. I could put up some shelves and line them all up. Then when a polio survivor calls me and asks for a word, I could help him find it. "You were talking about your mother in law, you say, and totally lost the word you were searching for. Does it start with a B? I have an entire shelf of B words. Bountiful? Good, I will send it right over."

I might need to hire a...hmmmmmm...they take letters......no, not Vanna White. She turns letters, but she doesn't actually take any. No, I mean those people with the pads...not bachelors...darn it, I know the word. Secretary, yes, I might need to hire a secretary to help me keep track of the...uh...you know...those things on the shelves in my new store. Words, that's what I was going to say. Words.

Resolutions, Schmesolutions!

It's that time of year again. I still have resolutions I have not used from the last millennium, but I think I'll try it one more time. Hard as it is for my loyal readers to believe, I have messed up at times in my life There are probably things I could do differently to better effect.

With that in mind, here are my Resolutions For 2015:
1. I will faithfully back up all my computer files. Having had my first hard drive failure since I started using computers back in 1993, I have learned my lesson.
2. I will kill no more petunias. Every spring, I plant some petunias, set them on my balcony and forget all about them. No more of that. I have bought my last bedding plant.
3. I will eat healthier meals, limiting my intake of sugar, fat and salt. (As soon as I get rid of all the Christmas goodies. I'm working hard on that!)
4. I will not wait till the day before my deadline to start thinking of what I can write in the newsletter.
5. I will limit my online time to fewer than 8 consecutive hours. Pinterest will have to get along without me for enough time to actually eat, sleep, and connect with non-cyber people.
6. I will avoid the Polio Wall by remembering to say NO sometimes and not always just in reply to questions beginning with "Would you mind..."
7. Naps are a good thing. I will reacquaint myself with that concept.
8. I will hug someone once a day. Everyone needs a daily hug. (I'll try to hug only people I already know, not accost strangers on the street.) 1
9. I will remember to maintain an attitude of gratitude. There is always something to be thankful for. Always.
10. I will seek out the company of people who make me laugh and will try to make at least one person a day smile.

That should keep me busy throughout the year. Whether or not I will last past April with these resolutions is questionable, but I will try. And I wish every one of you a new year that is filled with love, laughter, rest, pacing, pain-free days, healthy food and just enough trouble to keep you humble without causing you to despair.

Rules of Engagement

No, I'm not going to tell you how to get a big shiny diamond engagement ring. I am going to tell you how to win friends and influence people through your email posts, or at least how to avoid alienating the people with whom you correspond.

Rule #1. Be considerate of the feelings of others. If you wouldn't say this to someone sitting right in front of you, don't put it in your post and send it. If you feel you must send an angry post, write it, save it in your Drafts folder and look at it again the next day. You may have cooled off by then or realized you'd misunderstood.

Rule #2. Forwards...please don't. Those cute little things you get that tell you to send this to everyone you know or Jesus won't love you anymore or you will have bad luck or your hair will fall out in clumps...they are designed by spammers. You see it, you think it's cute, you hit Forward and all the addresses you put in, plus all the ones that were left on there when you got it go to spammers. Spammers think this is Christmas! What a gift! They can harvest those email addresses and send out spam or even viruses. Jesus may still love you, but your friend who has just gotten a virus may not.

Rule #3. If you get a post that makes your blood boil, listen carefully now, DO NOT REACT TO IT! If it angers you, it will anger the recipient of your post. Why would you do that to someone you like well enough to correspond with? Also, check with snopes.com or truthorfiction.com or any of the other fact checking sites online. And don't fall for that line at the bottom that says Checked with Snopes and it's true. Check for yourself. I've found that most of the blood boilers are false or only partly true or are political propaganda. Just because it says it has been checked does not necessarily mean it really has been. Is it hateful? If so, delete it. Save your blood pressure and that of your friends.

Rule #4. Try to use proper spelling. Most email clients have spell check. It's there for a reason. And using all caps means, in internet language, that you are shouting. Notice the caps in the above rule. Yes, I was shouting. I wanted to get your attention. But this entire article is not in caps.

Rule #5. When replying to a post, highlight the part you are responding to and then hit Reply. Only that portion of the text that you highlighted will appear in your post. If that doesn't work, then highlight the parts you don't want to include and hit Delete. That way, those of us who are still on dialup won't have to waste our precious online moments downloading all the other posts in that conversation.

Rule #6. Your delete key is your friend. If you disagree with someone on your email list, do not respond in anger. Delete the offensive post and let it go. On our polio list, some of us have very painful days and we might respond in a very negative and hurtful manner. Learn to read with your heart. These are your friends, try to remember that.

Rule #7. Bill Gates, Facebook, or the Good Fairy...none of these will pay you to forward anything. There is no way for them to track email and besides, they just wouldn't. Use your head for more than a hatrack.

Rule #8. It's fine for you to have a religion. It's fine for you to be devout. Just try to remember that not everyone in the world is a Christian, but everyone does have a right to their own beliefs. Their own. Not yours. The same way with politics. Some people are Republicans, some are Democrats, some don't even live in the US and could not care less about our politics. If you want to debate that sort of thing or the religious thing, join a group set up for that purpose. If a person wakes up with pain at level 7 on a 1-10 scale, they don't need to be bashed over the head with your political/religious beliefs. Our group is for support and information on how to deal with our PPS.

Rule #9. While online petitions might give notice to someone as to how a lot of people feel about a certain subject, they are not legal as a written petition is. Remember, I could have fifteen or more email addresses and send my signature from each one of them.

Rule #10. Remember to nurture your sense of humor. Laughter is the best possible exercise for a polio survivor. Don't react in anger, try to see the humor in every situation. I'm not recommending that you laugh in church, but even if you did, I don't think the Almighty would hold it against you.

SITTING PRETTY

One of my friends brought up an interesting subject. Well, interesting to me and my female readers mostly, I suppose. The question is this: How do you keep your knees together while sitting in your wheelchair if you don't have the muscle strength to do so? Perhaps men would like to look less splayed out, too, but for us women it is a modesty issue.

In the summer, I wear skirts rather than pants because I am always too warm. As opposed to the winter, when I'm always too cold. I was taught that it wasn't lady like to cross one's legs, but you could cross your ankles. That always brought vividly to mind the leader of a girl's group I belonged to in my teens. Those rules were vigorously applied in this organization, so the girl leading our group never crossed her legs. However, when she crossed her ankles, her knees were defiantly pointed away from each other. You know how rebellious teenage girls can be and this was an era when that was considered very rebellious indeed.

So what is the answer? Some people suggested a belt applied to the legs either above or just below the knees. If you are in your chair all the time, that might work for you. I know I would totally forget my knees were tied together and would stand up and fall on my face. It would prevent my usual fall, though. The one where my left leg goes straight out in front of me and I land on my much abused "good" knee. That has happened so often that I've had to install quotes around the word "good."

Perhaps a dot of stick-on Velcro applied to the inseam of one's pants? Duct tape? Maybe a pillow tucked in beside your thigh to force your legs closer together? I can tuck my polio affected ankle behind the other one and that keeps my knees together, but I can only hold that position so long before my legs go to sleep. At this point in my life, I can still remember that the ankle is trapped behind my other ankle, but I'm getting older and I can foresee a day when I'll forget even that. There could be a face plant in my future.

In the winter, a blanket over your legs solves the problem nicely and kills two birds with one stone, something I'm always in favor of. If anyone has a good solution to this problem, please let me know. For now, I will wear longer skirts in the summer. Not those beautiful gauzy full skirts I love so much, though. Nope. They get caught in my wheelchair's wheels and get torn off. When that happens, I have bigger problems than just keeping my knees together.

St. Louis and Beyond

This year was the Post Polio Health International Conference held at the Hyatt Regency by the Arch Hotel in St. Louis. I've wanted to attend one of these conferences for ages, but this year, thanks to the generosity of the Nebraska Polio Survivor Association for paying my registration fee and my friends Judy and Don Eades for supplying my transportation, I had my chance. I also volunteered to be a presenter on my favorite subject Humor Heals.

Once this conference was over, the Eadeses and I would head to Branson for the annual Internet Polio Reunion. All together, we would be gone 11 days. Therefore, on May 30, I got up at the unheard of hour of 4 AM. I had made arrangements with my granddaughter and a family friend to pick me up and take me to Omaha where I would meet up with Don and Judy, who would take it from there. Now I know how annoying I am when I always want to be early! However, Don and Judy were at our appointed meeting place when we arrived. I slept more than half the way to St. Louis.

Upon arriving at the hotel, I discovered that the woman I was sharing a room with had reserved her room and another one under another friend's name and there was no mention of me. A small panic attack later, both women arrived and we settled in.

There were about 5 presentations offered in each time slot, so Judy and I tried to split up and cover as many as possible with the idea of sharing with our polio groups at the end of the conference. I enjoyed most of the presentations. Statistics tend to make my eyes glaze over, so I nearly fell asleep at one presentation. The others took up the slack and I learned a lot.

For me, the best part was meeting other polio survivors, some of whom I'd known online for as long as 18 years, some I'd met in person, and others who were brand new to me. There were people who had read my column in Gleanings, the newsletter for Nebraska Polio Survivors Association, since its inception about 30 years ago. That was gratifying.

By the end of the conference, I was getting pretty ragged around the edges. We left St. Louis on Tuesday, June 3, and headed for Branson. My Branson group is not as structured as the PHI conference was, being more social than educational. Officially, it started on Friday, but many of us come in early to help set up, get the groceries for our noon meals, things like that. I was pleased to be there early enough that I could take a day to recuperate. I stayed in my room, listening to an audiobook and relaxing.

We had a wonderful time in Branson and if anyone of you would like to join us, it is held the second weekend of June every year. Contact me for more information (mil.lill@gmail.com). We had a therapist for a speaker and Randy Plummer performed for us one night. We also had a surprise story teller who donned a wolf costume and read to us about the other side of the story about the Big Bad Wolf and the Three Little Pigs. Apparently, it was all a big misunderanding and the wolf was the victim.

All in all, I've had a wonderful trip, reunited with old friends and made some new ones and even got another speaking engagement out of the deal. I will be talking to the Iowa Polio Survivors in Des Moines on October 19. I'm looking forward to it.

Standing Up For Yourself From a Seated Position

Probably it's a biological thing, discrimination. You would think that humanity had evolved beyond the kind of thinking that makes the odd colored baby chick get pecked to death by his peers, but apparently not.

I want to go on record as saying that where I live is a wonderful place to live, filled with terrific people who are kind, generous, accepting and fun loving. However, there are those few. You've met them, I know you have, or others just like them.

There's the Glamourous Guy, that good looking guy who wears starched and ironed, crisp white shirts every day and thinks our building needs to be ritzy. He doesn't like my chair, although he has no problems with me personally and if I would just stop being disabled and walk like a normal person, he might consider becoming friends with me. And as soon as he stops being judgmental and uppity, I might consider becoming friends with him. He thinks my chair makes this place look like a nursing home. I think he should have considered the fact that only seniors can live here and often that involves wheelchairs, walkers, canes and such. He'd be better off living with people he considers his peers. I'm thinking somewhere in Hollywood, where reality isn't so prevalent.

And there is the Owner. Since it is a Cooperative, we all own a piece of this building and it's furnishings. She, however, thinks of herself as the Boss of Us All. I'm not supposed to pull out a chair so that I can sit up to the table with my power chair in the Great Room. No, I'm not worthy of sitting up to the table as if I were a Real Person, I can just sort of crowd into a corner, or better yet, not join the other ladies at coffee at all. The one time I defied her, pulled out a chair and sat up to the table, she slammed down her coffee cup and stomped off to her apartment. She would prefer that we not talk to each other in the halls or on our decks because it might disturb her TV watching. Nothing we have to say could possibly be as important as Survivor or Big Brother! She does not have to pay any attention to the Handbook that explains procedure here, either. She's above all that nonsense.

The rest are Hangers On. They don't really know if they hate my chair or not, but The Owner tells them they do, so they do as they are told. There are not that many, but enough of them to make me spend an entire week in bed with migraines and heart palpitations. It was my own fault for letting them get to me like that. I know that I cannot control anyone else's actions, only my reactions, but when I was told that I cheated to get in here by 'sneaking in' my wheelchair, it was too much. It came from a woman I had not realized was a Hanger On and whom I'd thought was friendly to me. That made it very shocking to me. It was simply the last straw after three solid years of this kind of thing. I'd reached saturation point.

Thus it happened that at a Board Meeting where our Managing Agent explained the Fair Housing Act and passed out booklets that she had printed up with more detailed information, I lost it. Yep, level headed, I Can Take It, little old me. I just came right out with it. "What about this chair is bringing down property values?" I asked Glamour Guy. "I am getting tired of being told that the carpet is worth more than I am!" I told The Owner. I'd heard "If you can't walk, you can't live here" too many times. I asked if they would truly kick our oldest resident to the curb if she happened to break her hip. "Would you truly be that heartless" I asked, "to expect a 95 year old woman to have to pack up and move rather than recuperate in her own home?"

Normally, I keep quiet, avoid the bullies, stay out of the way and associate mostly with my polio survivor friends. But this time, I didn't. I felt I was doing this for more than just myself. After all, this building is under the Fair Housing Act and it is perfectly possible that another wheelchair user might someday move in.

I'd already been informed that The Owner had bullied a new resident to the point that this woman was afraid to join us for our monthly activities. That's just not right. No one should have that much power. So I spoke up. I raised my voice. I did not let the bullies win. Not this time. Not ever again. I cannot be evicted. I'm protected by the FHA. And I will continue to advocate for the disabled as I've been doing for over 20 years, even if that disabled person is myself.

TAKE WHAT YOU WANT AND PAY FOR IT

A friend of mine uses the phrase "energy tokens" to denote how much energy she has for the day. I like that. It reminds me, when I'm paying attention, that I have only so much energy and it is not something I can go to the bank and borrow more to get by. Nope, we get so many for today and that's it. If we rest, we will have the same amount tomorrow. Maybe.

Sometimes I get greedy and try to use all of my energy tokens for the week in one fell swoop. Not a good plan. Last week was just such an occasion. On Thursday, I had a visit with a grandson, followed by my book club, which I love so much. It was Easter week and traditionally, I help one of my great grandsons dye Easter eggs. It's such a delight to me and I realize that he will, in the blink of an eye, become too old for such. '

So I went to his house on Friday and helped dye eggs. Actually, I held his baby sister Kolbie while he and his mommy and my sister dyed eggs. Kolbie and I were in charge of telling Ryder that his eggs were beautiful. Kolbie is a very active and adorable ten-month old and I played with her, bouncing her on my knee, playing Upside Down Kolbie and generally having a very good time.

Can you hear the energy tokens..ka ching, ka ching, ka ching? It was a beautiful day, warm and sunny, and my granddaughter decided to grill some burgers. We stayed and ate burgers and hot dogs, baked beans, chips, the first BBQ of the year. I was tired when I got home, so I went to bed early. Saturday arrived and two of my grandsons were going to be at their parents' house for supper, so my sister and I had to be there. I so rarely see these two. One is a teacher who will be moving closer to home to teach in a nearby school this fall. The other is a college student who works for a Representative in the State House and is very busy all the time. That was also a fun night. Ka ching, ka ching, ka ching.

Sunday was Easter and my niece and her husband wanted to take me and my sister out to Easter Breakfast. Could I say no? Of course not! Another niece was there with her husband, son, and granddaughter and it was just lovely. More Ka ching of energy tokens disappearing.

At this point, I'd spent all my energy tokens for the next several days, but did I learn? No. Our brother had invited us to his house for an early dinner/late lunch with his family, so, with very little time to recuperate between fun times, we took off for the 25 mile drive to his house. Once there, I had a great time (ka ching, ka ching) playing with the dog and watching the kids hunt for Easter eggs.

Monday morning, I was so exhausted I could not get out of bed. I slept late, forced myself to get up and take care of my little dog, then back to bed for three more hours. I was so tired I was dizzy. I mentally cursed myself for spending so much irretrievable energy. If energy tokens were money, I felt I'd paid for a Caribbean cruise! But would I do it again? I'd love to say no, that I'd learned my lesson, since I am still paying for that cruise even now, but we both know me too well to get away with such a bald faced lie.

Some things are worth the price. One day very soon, my great grandchildren as well as my grandchildren will be beyond dyeing Easter eggs, playing Upside Down Kolbie and wanting to spend time with this doddering old lady. There will be time to rest then, one way or another. So I take what I want and pay for it.

The End and the Beginning

As I write this, New Years Eve is just a few days away. Goodbye old year, hello new year. This year has seen a few changes in my life. My sister sold her house and moved into the apartment next door to mine early this year. It has been great having her close by. Since she is 11 years older than I am, we really didn't get to know each other well until I was grown up. Then she raised her kids, I raised mine, I moved to Canada and I came back. She put up with my living in her house for the better part of a year while I searched for a place of my own. Now we share meals often, coffee nearly every morning. It's great.

There were other changes as well. My youngest grandson has decided to go into politics, which has been his passion for a long while. In June, he will try for the nomination of State Representative for our district. He's worked in the State House in Des Moines for four years now and loves it. Unfortunately for me, this means that his tenure as my personal slave is over. Back in the day, he was my 'go to' guy for setting up my Christmas tree, putting it away again, and numerous other chores. Not any more.

I guess one thing I must learn in the coming year is to Ask For Help. Oh no. The hardest thing in this world for me or most polio survivors is to Ask For Help. I have never minded asking my grandkids, because all modesty aside, they adore me. They are always willing to help, but this one is now a 2 hr. drive away and seems to want a life of his own.

I have other grandchildren, but they have jobs and/or families to attend to. I think I must wean myself off them and learn to ask others. We do have a maintenance man here at Realife, plus my nephew lives just down the hall. Our Resident Service Director would be happy to help out in a pinch. I am also a member of a very large extended family, any of whom would probably help if I did get myself to AFH.

Usually, I don't make New Years resolutions because I have tons of them from years gone by that have never been used. Some are still in their shrink wrap, tags attached. However, this year will be the year that I resolve to learn to AFH when I need it. Unless I can figure out how to do it myself. No, no! I WILL AHF. Maybe. It's very difficult. If only these grandkids weren't so determined to grow up, get jobs and spouses and homes of their own. It messes up their priorities!

Learn from my mistakes, my friends. Really, it isn't so bad to Ask For Help. People feel good after doing something nice for someone else. Give them that gift from time to time. Trust me, the world will keep on twirling even if you don't do it all yourself. And it just might prevent you from overdoing to the point that you need even more help.

I hope the new year is a great year for all of us. Take care of yourselves and you might want to resolve to learn a new trick. I suggest it be AFH.

THE END IS NEAR

The end of 2012, I mean. Oh, did you think I was talking about that Mayan thing? No, I am sure they were wrong. If you are reading this, they definitely were wrong! I read somewhere that the Mayans did not figure in leap years, so if that is true we are already well past December 21, 2012.

This has been a good year for me. I started doing an online monthly polio newsletter for postpoliobransongoers.org and am enjoying that a lot as well as my bi-monthly column for Gleanings. Combined with a poem every month for my poetry group, this keeps me busy and out of trouble. Mostly. My family has also gained its first girl born into our family in 25 years. Kolbie Lou Kalani Malone, welcome to the mayhem that is our family.

There is so much information online about post polio and so many online support groups. I belong to several email lists and several Facebook pages, all for polio survivors. I've learned so much from these groups. In case any of you are interested in the Facebook forums, here is a list. Just go to the search bar on Facebook and type in these names. Some are closed groups, meaning that even though anyone can see the names of members, only members can read what is on those pages, while others are open groups. Posts in open groups can be read by anyone.

Post Polio is a closed group. Click on the About tab and you can see if a group is Open or Closed. Harvest Center's Post Polio Coffee House is an Open group started by Dr. Richard Bruno. Post Polio Syndrome is an open group. Post-Polio Network RSA is a closed group. The RSA stands for Republic of South Africa. Some of you might know Cilla Webster from South Africa. This is her group. Power Chairs R Great is an open group that is meant for discussion of power chairs and our experiences with them. Land of The Sky Post-Polio Support Group is another Open group. Polio History is an Open group. There are probably even more out there, but I find that reading the posts on these keeps me pretty busy. It is just good to know that we are not alone, that whatever problems we are experiencing, someone has been there, done that and will listen without judging.

One of my online friends, Cindy Koshinski Bernstein posted this and I asked if I could share it. She said it came from a friend of hers and they didn't know the author:

10 COMMANDMENTS FOR REDUCING STRESS IN YOUR LIFE
1. Thou Shalt Not Be Perfect, Or Even Try To Be
2. Thou Shalt Not Try To Be All Things To All People.
3. Thou Shalt Sometimes Leave Things Undone That Ought To Be Done.
4. Thou Shalt Not Spread Thyself Too Thinly.
5. Thou Shalt Learn To Say No.
6. Thou Shalt Schedule Time For Thyself And Thy Supportive Network.
7. Thou Shalt Switch Off And Do Nothing Regularly.
8. Thou Shalt Be Boring, Untidy, Inelegant, and Unattractive At Times.
9. Thou Shalt Not Even Feel Guilty.
10. Especially, Thou Shalt Not Be Thine Own Worst Enemy But Be Thine Own Best Friend.

I will leave you with these commandments and my sincere wishes for a wonderful 2013, filled with love, laughter, and friendship. Remember to Conserve to Preserve.

The Latest Trip

I left Iowa on October 3, 2000. Carolann and I went first to Minnesota to visit a polio pal up there, then headed back to Waterloo,Iowa to retrieve a donated scooter that another polio pal had found on the Internet. Just as we pulled into Waterloo, the engine on my van started to overheat. With help from the man who donated the scooter, we found a 24 hour mechanic and were soon on our way.

October 14 and 15 found us attending a polio conference sponsored by the Ontario March of Dimes and held in the Sheraton Hotel in Hamilton, Ontario. The conference was not heavily attended, but I did meet some interesting people and heard some good presentations.

On October 15, I was one of the speakers. I spoke on the topic "Humor Heals." This was my first time presenting anything and I was a little nervous, but it went over fairly well. I hope to do this again sometime.

After attending a friend's wedding, and delivering the scooter, Carolann and I started the trip south. We left November2, first stop Baltimore, MD. Sheila Tohn, a friend of ours, had moved into a nursing home there and we wanted to visit.

A nursing home has always been one of the boogie-men in my Closet of Fears. But Sheila's is nice. She has her own room, the staff is not only helpful and friendly, but there are actually enough of them employed to do a good job. This nursing home is also trying out the Eden Principle, wherein the residents are in an environment with young children (the employees have a Day Care center in the building and the residents are encouraged to interact with the kids) and are allowed pets. There are lots of activities, too.

From Baltimore, we traveled along the edge of Washington, D.C. We briefly toyed with the idea of touring the capital, but hurriedly gave it up once we discovered that the drivers in that area are homicidal maniacs, hell bent on smashing into someone (us, apparently, for choice) before they quit for the night. I locked the keys in the van while we had a cup of coffee at an International House of Pancakes, and the cop who retrieved them for us suggested we NOT stay the night in that area. We took his suggestion and moved along.

We did get a chance to look Alexandria, VA over a bit (mostly because we got lost there) and found it to be a lovely but totally inaccessible place.

Next stop, Petersburg, VA. My brother and his wife hosted us for a couple of days while we rested and ate some of my sister in law's delicious cooking. She is of German descent and cooks like an angel. The water pump went out of the van while we were on our way out of Petersburg, necessitating a five hour delay, spent cooling our heels in a Pep Boys.

After Petersburg, we headed for Florida. En route, we got distracted and spent a few hours in beautiful Savannah, GA. We got out our power chairs and wandered along the riverfront for a couple of hours. Savannah is very lovely. Most of the little shops along the riverfront were, you guessed it, inaccessible, but not the Praline Shop! MMMmmmmmmmmmmmmm.

On to Florida for a brief visit with Helen Ferguson, a polio pal who lives in Jacksonville. We had lunch with her and a nice visit, then went to Trenton, FL for a longer visit with Art and Nancy Coburn. We stayed there for 5 days, during which time we made a side trip to St. Augustine and toured the art gallery and the ancient fort. The weather was great and the power chairs made the excursion most enjoyable.

After bidding a fond farewell to the Coburns, we tooled on down the highway to Lafayette, LA for a week with Jane Bercier, including a Cajun Thanksgiving. I split the skin on the bottom of my heel while I was there, so we didn't do much but loll around and visit and eat Cajun food. One afternoon was spent in New Orleans, my favorite city, touring the French Quarter, the French Market and Cafe du Monde for cafe au lait, beignet and jazz.

Then on to Austin, TX. Marsha Coleman was our hostess there for a few days. While we were there, we attended an ADAPT meeting. ADAPT is a disability rights organization that really works hard to make sure the ADA is taken seriously.

From Austin, we traveled north to Dallas, TX for a couple of days with David Brock and his family. David is the person in charge of one of the Internet support groups to which I belong and is also a dear friend.

We left Dallas on Saturday, December 2 and were about an hour and a half away when the transmission went out of my van. Never doubt that we have a guardian angel, though, because the tranny went out while on a slight downhill slope. Carolann,who was driving, coasted down that hill, onto the off ramp and right into the driveway of a Chrysler/Plymouth Auto Plex. There was just enough "go" left in the transmission to get us into the service bay, (only an hour and a half before closing time, I might add) and not one inch further.

The people at the Glenn Polk Auto Plex in Gainesville, TX were wonderful. They helped us find a motel, negotiated a reasonable room rate, moved our gear to the motel and lent us a brand new van till Monday morning. We could then get some food in and make ourselves at home in the motel. We were there four days and three nights. Boring!!

When we finally got out of Gainesville, we headed for St. Louis. While there, we had a nice telephone chat with a polio pal who is also undergoing cancer treatment.

Finally, on Thursday, December 7, nearing midnight, we pulled into my drive. The snow waited till we got in the house before doing its thing. I had seen the skylines of many cities on this trip, but the seven or eight streetlights of Dow City, IA put them all to shame in my book.

BIG CITY LIGHTS

Most of my friends seem to live in big cities or very urban areas. I, on the other hand, have lived my entire life in small town mid-America. This makes for some interesting conversations. I will mention a movie I'd love to see. "Run down to Blockbuster and rent it. It's well worth it," my friend from Los Angeles suggested.
"Uh...Blockbuster is in Omaha, 65 miles away. By the time I drive there, rent the movie, come home...it's too late to watch the movie and get it back in time to avoid a late charge."

When I was trying to decide what sort of door to put in to gain access to my new deck, another friend mentioned a triple fold glass door that she had really admired. "Your local door store should have one like it," she mentioned. Yes, my local door store. I live in a town of 450 people. We don't even have a grocery store! The aforementioned Omaha might possibly have a door store, but I wouldn't have the foggiest idea of where it would be.

On the other hand, when I mentioned that my local mini-mart was robbed by a young man who grew up here, my friends were quite surprised that everyone in the mini mart knew him, even with a ski mask over his very familiar face. "They recognized his mother's car," I told them. "All the cops had to do was drive to his mother's house (everyone knew where she lived, of course) and arrest him."

During my first few months of widowhood, I applied for Social Security, told the official to have the check direct deposited and gave him all the relevant information allowing him to do so. I then made out and mailed checks to pay my bills for that month and went to visit my sister in Michigan for a couple of weeks.

Arriving home, I retrieved my mail and to my horror, there was my Social Security check! All those checks I'd written...I was sure I didn't have enough in my account to cover them all. I trudged dispiritedly to my bank to get the bad news.

"Oh, not to worry," my banker told me. "I knew this was probably what happened, so I just forwarded enough money from your farm account to cover your checks." This was the vice president of the local branch of my bank.

And what about the time my grandson David rented an apartment in Phoenix and used me (with my permission) as a reference? His realtor called my bank to check up on me, to see if I could cover David's rent if he failed to pay up. This time, before she would give out any information on me, the vice president of the bank called my house to get my permission. My line was busy, so she hopped in her car, came to my house, and asked me in person. Do you get that kind of service in a city? Don't think so!

Cities have much to recommend them. Shopping is easier and more varied, there are many forms of entertainment available and job opportunities abound. But I'll stay in my little niche in rural Iowa, surrounded by townsfolk who know me, my family, and my business, even at the risk of being the center of town gossip on the odd occasion.

THE LITTLE SCOOTER THAT COULD

At the July meeting of NPSA, we had a real Pay It Forward moment. Here's how it happened: Gleason Grimes, a now-deceased member of NPSA, bought a folding scooter to enable him and his wife Pat to travel. This scooter would fold up like a suitcase, small enough to fit in the trunk of a car and could also be carried safely on an airplane. It does not come apart, except for the batteries, which are easily removable.

When Gleason died, Pat sold this scooter to her cousin, Phil Vrana, also an NPSA member. Recently Phil also passed on. His children wanted to donate his mobility equipment to polio survivors like their father, so now The Scooter was back in circulation.

Tom Skarin, polio survivor, was in need of a a travel scooter that would fit in the trunk of his small car. Tom is a friend of mine and so is Pat Grimes, who was in contact with the her cousins, the Vranas. I asked Pat to ask Phil's family if Tom could have the scooter and, thus, the scooter became Tom's.

However, there were logistics to work out: the scooter was now in Pat's home in Milford, Nebraska. Pat drove from Milford to the meeting place at Bloomfield Forum in Omaha for the July NPSA meeting and the scooter was handed off to Tom, who had driven from his home in Ida Grove, Iowa.

Now Tom can go to the Omaha zoo, to the Clay County Fair in Spencer, Iowa, and to the sculpture garden in Des Moines. Tom will pay it forward by driving Millie to Omaha for the NPSA meeting in August. Pay It Forward is such a satisfying concept. I recommend it heartily.

THIRTY YEARS: WHAT NPSA HAS MEANT TO ME

The Nebraska Polio Survivor Association was founded thirty years ago by Nancy Baldwin Carter. It has been a major factor in my life for nearly that long.

I remember the first time I heard of Post-Polio Syndrome. My husband was undergoing some tests in the hospital and I was in the waiting room. I saw a brochure from NPSA, and, curious, I picked it up and read it. I was stunned. It described exactly what I'd been going through, the frequent falls, the muscle pain, and the fatigue. Up until then, I'd had no idea why this was happening to me. I called Nancy and we talked. She gave me the name of a doctor who specialized in PPS.

After I'd seen this doctor, I spoke to Nancy again. Then I started sending in articles for Gleanings. Soon I found myself the editor of this newsletter. At that time, Gleanings went out to over 2000 readers in several countries.

Nancy's successor, Marian Barnett, helped me with editing the newsletter, formatting it and getting it ready to print. In 1993, my husband died and I was too overwhelmed to continue editing the newsletter, so I turned it over to Marian. I became a contributing editor and have been steadily churning out the columns ever since.

My column in Gleanings has led me to a new life. I had no idea there were so many of us, as I'd never met another polio survivor. But through Gleanings and, later, with the advent of the Internet, I met many more, some in person, some online. Dr. Richard Bruno followed my column and convinced me to put my columns into a book, which I did. I did a bit of public speaking at polio conferences in Canada and the U. S. Through that exercise, I met more polio survivors, some of whom felt they knew me because they'd been reading my column for so long.

In 1996, and for several years after, I traveled with an online friend. We met polio survivors all over the US and Canada. In almost every case, it was as though we'd known each other forever. We had so much in common. We had enough differences to make us interesting, but enough similarities to create a bond. Those were such wonderful times.

We had no money to speak of, so we camped in the minivan, cooked our meals at rest areas, and met these wonderful people, many of whom are still close friends.

I married my now ex-husband in Branson, Missouri, at our annual Polio Reunion. David Brock, a very dear friend and fellow polio survivor, performed our ceremony over a web cam and speaker phone. David was too fragile to travel from his home in Bedford, Texas to Branson. Except for my granddaughter, my bridesmaids were all polio survivors. Except for the best man, so were the groomsmen. The music was provided by more polio survivors.

Although the marriage did not last, that wedding was wonderful. No nerves, because I knew that anything that went wrong would just make us all laugh. There was so much love in that room. My polio survivor friends are my other family and I love them dearly.

Is it any wonder that I always say that having had polio is as much blessing as curse? I firmly believe that my life would not have been half as rich and fulfilling if I had not met my polio family.

I look forward every month to the meetings of NPSA in Omaha, seeing old friends, meeting new ones, hearing the speakers that our executive director, Elaine Alien, finds for us and feeling the comfort of being with people who have been there, done that and don't see me as different.

If you have never attended a meeting of NPSA and live in the area, I urge you to join us on the first Sunday of every month except December and January. We meet at 2:00 PM at Bloomfield Forum, at 98th and Nicholas in Omaha, Nebraska.

Tipping the Scales

For years, I have had a feud with my body. It never seems to be quite right for the occasion. After polio, I was far too thin. Then, after a 2 month stint in a wheelchair at age 10, I was too fat. In high school, I was not pretty enough. As a young mother of three very active little boys, my body did not seem to have enough energy to get through my day. It wasn't just my muscles and skeleton that displeased me, it was my face, my figure, my hair, my fingernails. It seemed that no matter how hard my poor body worked, it just couldn't please me.

Slowly, my body and I are reaching detente. I have given up the fight to have a stylish hairdo. My hair will spitefully grow an inch immediately after being permed, resulting in a flat spot with fuzzy ends. It has no texture, is very slick, and has been known to spit bobby pins across the room in protest of my trying to force it into a French Roll. So I wear it in a simple style that requires no perm, no curlers, no deadly bobby pins.

The fact that I'm short has also ceased to cause me great distress. I have tall grandsons who can change light bulbs for me or reach the good dishes down from the top cupboard shelf. I have heard every short joke ever told, although I am not really all that short. I know at least two people who are shorter than I am. My mother was only 4'7" when she died at nearly 98. I spend a lot of time in my wheelchair now, so height is pretty much immaterial at this point.

My fingernails, oh how I've longed for beautiful hands with long, glossy nails. Not gonna happen. I can grow hair, but not fingernails. So I keep them cut short and remember that my hands may not be beautiful, but they are capable. And which would you rather have anyway, I ask myself, pretty hands or useful hands. Both, I retort. But I'll settle for useful.

Weight. Ah, that bugaboo that haunts all women and almost all polio survivors regardless of gender. Before I moved from Canada, 1 had the perfect bathroom scale. It was rusted to the point that everyone, from my 6'3" husband to my little Papillon dog, weighed 160 Ibs. It made everyone feel good. My husband felt svelte, my dog felt big and ferocious (something she has aimed for all her life) and I was not terribly displeased, although 160 is still too much for my smallish frame.

But alas, all good things come to an end. I didn't bring that scale with me when I moved. I bought a new one, but not one of those talking ones. I hate those even more than the other kind. I step on the talking scale and it says, "One at a time, please!" So rude. The one I bought is in cahoots with my doctor's scale. They both tell me the same sad story. They lie, of course, but I'm used to that. My birth certificate tries to tell people that I'm old, too.

Losing weight is nearly impossible for a polio survivor who spends a lot of time in a wheelchair. I do try to move as much as I can but it's a tightrope I must walk. Too much exercise and I'm so fatigued that I need to sleep for a day, thus getting no exercise at all that day. Too little and I am deconditioned and will gain weight. Therefore, I have given up all hope of being Miss America...I think you have to be tall for that, anyway...and have learned to live with my rather squat, toad-like physique. After all, if you believe my birth certificate, and I urge you not to, I'm an old woman, so who really cares how I look. I have inner beauty. "Must be," my smart aleck sons tell me. My appearance seems to please my grandchildren and great grandchildren, because they sure light up when they see me. And that makes me feel very beautiful.

Yes, we've reached detente, my body and I. I realize that it has done a pretty darn good job over all these years, and while working with decidedly less than wonderful equipment. Mismatched legs and feet, lungs that tend to wheeze when stressed, arms that are not very strong. The legs bend to make a great lap for my great grandchildren and the arms are just right for hugs. My lungs fill up with sweet baby smells and I am content.

TIRED OF BEING FATIGUED

There has been a lot of discussion about fatigue on my favorite Facebook pages. As polio survivors, most of us have Type A personalities, which makes resting difficult. If we treat our fatigue by resting, we fear that people will see us as lazy. Have you ever met a lazy Type A person? Neither have I. Nor a lazy polio survivor, for that matter.

Dr. Bruno said that when the polio virus hit, it shotgunned throughout our systems, and one of the casualties of that war is the hypothalamus gland, if I remember correctly. And that would be some kind of miracle, wouldn't it? But let's suppose I'm right. That gland, as I understand it, is the 'brakes' in our brain. As an example, let's say there is a five car pileup. One of the survivors of this wreck is a polio survivor. The rest are able bodied, but there are bumps, contusions, fractures involved in all of the people involved. Guess who will still show up for work and even apologize for being late? Yep. A polio survivor will crawl to work on bloody stumps where a normal person would call in sick. A pristine, undamaged hypothalamus gland would have put the brakes on, sent the message to the brain that we are hurt and need to rest. We need that, but we don't have that.

There is also the fact that so many of us just don't look disabled. In my case, I am healthy as a horse, have a happy attitude and usually have a smile on my face. This leads people to think that I am faking and using my chair because "everything is easier from a chair." This quote is obviously from someone who has never had to do everything from a chair. One day, I wore a skirt, my brace blatantly on display. Several people asked what happened to my leg. Yes, these were the same people who thought I was faking. I told them that I've worn the brace for years and years because I'd had polio as a child.

Another time, I slipped down to get my mail in my slippers and pajamas. There is always someone out in the hall on those occasions, isn't there? Without my brace, my polio affected leg is noticeably smaller and my foot is obviously deformed. Another person shocked. I'm not faking, how about that.

I've met so many polio survivors over the years, because this is my favorite demographic. Most of them have been the 'go to' people in their families. When disability hits, these very active polio survivors have to explain their fatigue to people who are used to seeing them as tireless workers. "But you've always...(fill in your exhausting job of choice here). Who can we get to do that now?" we hear. "It isn't that big a job. It's only five or six hours, surely you can do that?"

Part of the problem is that the treatment for polio is the exact opposite of the treatment for PPS. When we were in the rehabilitation stage of our recovery, we needed to work hard to get those little motor neurons to sprout and enervate the orphaned muscles that were left with no motor neurons to call their own. So we did. We exercised, we learned to roller skate, we danced, we held down full time jobs, we married, we raised families. But when PPS hit, and it does hit about 85% of us, we were so used to the go-go-go lifestyle that slowing down was just alien to us.

Conserve to Preserve. Totally new idea. People will think we are lazy! I don't want to look like a cripple! I don't want people to feel sorry for me! Since that damaged hypothalamus is of no help in this situation, we have to consciously reset our thinking. We must go from the mantra for able bodied people, Use it or Lose it, to the PPS mantra, Overuse it and you WILL lose it.

When the polio virus hit our spinal column, it wiped out about 50% of our motor neurons, 60% in any limb that was paralyzed. So we are starting out with a deficit. Aging kills off more neurons and most of ours have divided themselves in the rehab part of our recovery, making them less sturdy than a normal neuron. Oh oh, it doesn't take much to kill off those damaged neurons and then where are we?

We have muscles that have, in essence, been unplugged from our brains. It's like when the internet goes down...no signal. Except that once the neuron is dead, that's it. No techie to call to fix it.

All of this is just to try to get my polio survivor friends to realize that we truly do need to slow down. It's OK to say No. Really. I tried it once and the world kept on twirling exactly the same as it had when I was doing every job set in front of me. Amazing, huh?

If there is a job you feel you simply have to do, try breaking it down into small chunks. Let's say the laundry has to be done because you have put it off till you have no clean clothes at all. Very few of us are in the age group that would make nudity an option. Break the job down. Sort the clothes. Rest. Put the clothes in the washer and while they are washing, sit down and put your feet up. DO NOT use that time to do another chore. Never mind efficiency, we are just trying to get the laundry done without spending the next day in bed, out of our minds on pain meds. Put that load in the dryer. Rest. Fold the clothes and put them back in the basket. Rest. I don't care what your mother told you, the clothes can be worn unironed and they can be used right out of that basket without making the transition to dresser drawer or closet. Tomorrow, if you want to, you can put the clothes away.

It is OK to be a little bit lazy. We've worked hard all our lives. Harder than able bodied people because it takes three times the energy for us to the same job as an able bodied person. So now we are entitled to take life three times as easy. Works for me.

TOLD YOU SO

I learned a new word the other day: Omnishambles. . Omni means all, and a quick glance around my apartment would tell you what shambles means. That word perfectly describes what my life was during May.

As you know, I like to keep busy. During a normal month, I do the online newsletter Polio Perspective and a column for Gleanings. I do the monthly calendar, newsletter, and word search puzzle for Realife, the cooperative where I live. I belong to a book club and a poetry group, both of which meet the last part of each month. May also had me designing a new brochure for Realife in time for our May 28 Open House and preparing to present a speech at the June 2nd meeting of NPSA as well as doing some rewriting and reformatting on my soon-to-be-published e-book version of Hot Water, Orange Juice and Kids.

Even when you add in the fact that I live pretty much in the middle of a 22-member, closely-knit family, all of whom insist on having birthdays and anniversaries from time to time and sometimes the odd potluck supper, I manage. Sometimes I manage better than other times.

This May was certainly the exception. I was doing fine with Pacing, Conserving to Preserve and all of the stuff I keep yammering at you guys to do and which I often fail to do myself. Then my brother-in-law died. His children and grandchildren came from New York and California to attend his funeral and to empty out his apartment and square away those things that await all of us.

First we had the funeral, then all the occasions to get together with this part of the family that we so rarely see, and I didn't want to miss out on any of it. However, deadlines were piling up. Fatigue had set up shop in my life and most of the time my ears were buzzing with it. One night I was in bed by 6 PM and did not waken till 8 AM the next day. Even so, I was exhausted. I didn't just hit the Polio Wall, I ran headlong into it and knocked myself cuckoo.

Somehow, I managed to get all of it done. I'm a perfectionist when it comes to my writing and I worried that the fatigue would cause me to make mistakes. I had purchased a travel scooter in preparation to riding along to Branson, Missouri, with some friends on June 6, planning to attend our annual polio reunion there. I'd only missed this reunion twice in the 14 years it has been going on. My registration fee was paid, my room reserved at the hotel.

Well, folks, I had to make a decision. Did I really want to go to Branson already exhausted? It would cost me between $400 and $500 all told, counting my registration fee, the hotel room, the gas and incidentals while there. That's a lot of money to spend on a three day nap, which is what it would have turned into. I wanted to go so badly, but I knew that the fatigue I was experiencing would make it a situation I endured rather than enjoyed. I canceled the trip.

June is being spent in a more relaxing fashion. I'm doing my columns ahead of deadline for a change and spreading out the rest of my activities. Please, people, do as I say, not as I do. Keep that Polio Dragon from biting you in the behind!

VOTE FOR ME

There's no getting around it, I am going to have to run for president of the US. Neither party has addressed the issues that need to be dealt with so I guess it's up to me. I will run, okay, roll on the PPS Reform ticket. Here are some of the changes I will make if you elect me your president.

February is gone. No more February. The year will go directly from January to March, the months of May, June, July, and August will each have five weeks. Winter is just too long for us cold-intolerant polio survivors. (Don't tell me I can't do this. Wasn't it one of the Caesars who thought up this whole calendar thing in the first place? If you thought Julius Caesar was a tough dude, it is obvious you have never had much dealings with your average polio survivor!)

The new technology will be immediately put to good use. Every household will have a "beamer upper." No more sitting hours and hours in airports, bus depots, train stations, no more fuming in traffic jams. A little button, a few words (Beam me up, Scottie) and you are home/at the office/at the beach.

Mall racing in power wheelchairs/scooters will be an Olympic event.

Money will be made available for research into the manufacture of easily affordable bionic parts. Your leg doesn't work this morning? Send it back to the factory and get a rebate on a brand new one, sleek, elegant and fully functional. (Of course, with my luck, I could only afford one, but my legs have never matched anyhow, so I doubt if I'd even notice.)

The US will be downsized. You know we have states we don't even use. Why should those two people have all of North Dakota to themselves, while Wyoming has only three or four people in it. We will combine those two, call it Wykota and the residents can just learn to share. For that matter, why do we need a North Dakota and a South Dakota, a North Carolina and a South Carolina, a West Virginia and a plain brown wrapper Virginia? That is ridiculous. If I' m elected, I will combine both halves of each state into one. So there will be a Dakota, a Virginia, a Carolina. This will cut down on the number of congressmen in Washington, D. C. (which will have, of course, been combined with Washington State) and make a huge savings in the cost of running our country. Fewer politicians can only be a good thing.

All military forces must be nude. World wide. No exceptions. I think a war conducted by totally nude soldiers armed only with silly string and supersoakers would have a much better chance of success than the methods tried so far. Beating people over the heads with clubs has not worked, shooting them full of arrows has not worked. Dropping atomic bombs on them has not had a noticeably good effect. Let's just give this nudity thing a try. If it doesn't work after the first war, we can always go back to the blood and guts method.

All architects will be required to use a wheel-chair full time while designing public buildings. No exceptions, no time off, no leaving the chair.

All wheelchairs will be equipped with a How Do You Like It button that turns rude people into paraplegics for twenty-four hours.

All government offices will be run exclusively by volunteer workers. No pay. No administrative expenses, no perks. No limos unless the volunteer happens to own his/her own. No private jets, no secret service men. The US will be run almost exclusively by middle aged women, as, indeed it nearly is now. Except now these women will be given the credit they deserve.

We will adapt the "hand in your gun" campaign to include

weapons of war. If you turn in a tank, you will get a bright red Mary Kay car and a year's worth of free lipstick. (I did mention that the New World will be run by women, didn't I? Oh, well, it will.) A missile will get you 5,000 Green Stamps to spend as you like. A nuclear warhead would get you a weekend with Tom Selleck. (Hmmmmmm. Where did I put that darn nuclear warhead? I really hate this PPS fog sometimes!)

Don't forget to vote, folks. If you don't vote, you can't complain. And I for one am not giving up my most cherished American freedom, the right to whine and fuss about the people in office.

When the Going Gets Tough

Today I got a letter from an older cousin. His wife has cancer and he is her caregiver. My sister has cancer, the other sister's husband has cancer. I belong to a large Internet support group of polio survivors with whom I am in daily contact. Most, if not all, of them are in varying degrees of decline and many are in deep physical and emotional pain. Sounds depressing, doesn't it?

Do you know what impresses me the most about all of these people? It is their courage and sense of humor and loving hearts. My cousin does not feel put upon by having to care for his wife. Yes, he is sad for her to be going through all this, but he feels privileged to be able to care for this woman he has loved for so many years. My sister and her husband have forged an even closer bond in an already loving marriage. The other sister has become more precious to us and remains our loving and often silly companion.

Almost daily, I hear of spouses asking for divorce when the other partner becomes disabled. It saddens me that these people do not know the joy of caring for a loved one. I am sad for the deserted disabled spouse also, but not as much as I am for the one who has left. He/she will never have the immense satisfaction of knowing that they are doing what they promised to do in their marriage vows and doing it willingly and with a loving heart. Knowing that the time together is limited gives the relationship a special poignancy that makes each moment together memorable.

WHAT DID YOU DO TO YOURSELF?

Have you ever gotten that question? When I first gave up the idea of keeping my brace covered by pants all the time, I heard this a lot. I was waitressing at the time. In Iowa. In the summer. In a building too old and drafty for A/C to be reliable. I decided to wear walking shorts. It was a good decision in one way because it was so much cooler. Nevertheless, people who had known me for years and surely must have noticed that I list noticeably to port and limp when I walk, had never seen my brace. I often wonder what reason they gave themselves for my obvious handicap.

"I didn't do anything to myself," I would say, somewhat affronted that people would think I'd deliberately damage my body, causing all this bother. "I had polio when I was four. Now I have Post Polio."

This usually got a strange stare. Sometimes, if we weren't busy, and since it was a small café in a small town we often weren't, I'd try to explain PPS. "Look," I'd say. "When the polio virus attacked my spinal cord, it destroyed about half or more of the motor neurons that send messages to the brain. Kind of like a spark plug wire. New little neurons sprouted from the remaining neurons and sorta kinda worked for awhile. Then the old neurons got worn out from doing all the work and the newer ones were not that strong to begin with, so here I am. I've come unplugged." That was usually all I had time to say.

These people were my neighbors and casual acquaintances. I didn't want to offend them by getting huffy, but neither did I want to go into a lot of detail to people who most likely weren't all that interested to start with.

Sometimes someone would see me using my power chair and would be puzzled because they'd seen me walking earlier that day, week, or month. Then I'd get , "Oh no! What did you do to yourself?" I would have to explain that I can only take a limited number of steps a day and that I was saving them for when I could not use the chair.

And then there would be times when I couldn't get my power chair in the store because of a step or too high threshold, so I'd park the chair and walk in. At that point, I got the "It's a miracle!" reaction. "I'm so glad to see you don't need that awful chair anymore. You look so much better today. I bet you are glad to get rid of that chair!" I think this reaction is harder to take than the what-did-you-do-toyourself stuff.

It seems so self pitying to tell people that you are walking because you have to, being unable to get into the store otherwise, and that you would be paying for this little walk big time. As far as that part about looking better without the chair...come on, how could I look better with my face squinched up in pain, breath coming in gasps, sweat running off my brow? Oh, wait. I'm forgetting. We polio survivors are so well trained in hiding our pain and difficulty that it is entirely possible no one can see how bad I'm hurting. Of course, there is no way they can tell that tomorrow or more likely the day after, I will be screaming in agony from leg spasms or, alternatively, woozy and disoriented from pain pills.

I would love to be able to say that once I'd explained all of this to people, they'd understand and I wouldn't have to do it again. Not so. It isn't only ordinary people who react this way, either. I've had mixed responses to the use of my chair from medical professionals and their staff, as well. I'd had a new brace made and came back in to the office for an adjustment. I was in my power chair. The receptionist, a perky little gal with, I want to emphasize, no medical training at all, told me to get out of that chair at once!

"Excuse me?" I said.

"We made you a brace so you don't have to use that chair anymore. Now get out of it at once!" Now, here's the thing...I've been a Mom for a very very long while and I don't take disrespect sitting down, even when I am sitting down. As you can imagine, this did not go over well. Lead balloon type of going over.

"Little girl," I told her, maintaining eye contact, "I am a polio survivor with about 200 steps a day at my disposal. I've used them all up by now. Furthermore, where I sit and how I get around are not your problem." She got a bit red in the face, but she did back down. She was extremely lucky that my mother gave me a good bringing up, although I often think that was a bigger handicap than polio provided.

I've heard all the "use it or lose it" nonsense I ever want to hear. I've had PPS for about 30 years now and I think I am a better judge of what works for me than someone who either just met me or has seen me only a few times. I do as much as I can, but I've learned when to quit.

If you are asked, "What did you do to yourself?" you have my permission to smile and say, "I learned how to live with PPS, whatever it takes." If you should happen to back over someone's toes during your retreat, absolutely by accident, of course, well...stuff happens, doesn't it.

You May Be A Polio Survivor IF...

1. You had polio and survived it. Duh. 1
2. You start to talk and, in mid-sentence, lose track of what you were saying. (This happens to mothers of small children, too, because of not being able to talk and monitor the area at the same time. The difference is, polio survivors will do this when there are no children around.)
3. Your startle reflex is so strong that you have installed Velcro on your chair to keep you from going airborne.
4. You fall in your living room and use that down time to take a nap.
5. You buy battery operated heated socks intended for hunters, but wear them inside all the time. Even with shorts and a halter top.
6. You can remember your polio experience vividly, but have difficulty remembering the names of your kids. You might have to check your driver's license from time to time to remember your own name.
7. You haven't been the right temperature for so long, you forget what it's like.
8. Your spouse wears thick socks to bed so your icy feet won't awaken him/her when you cuddle up.
9. You consider getting a T-shirt that reads, "Yes, I am drunk. That's why I list to port when I walk. I don't have Post Polio Syndrome, there's no such thing. Go away."
10. You have your house arranged so that everything is accessible from your wheelchair except the one thing you really need and no one else is home today.
11. You have days when you feel wonderful, full of pep and energy. Unfortunately, because you use those days to pretend you have never heard of PPS, they are usually followed by several days in bed unable to move.
12. You have heard the question, "Why do you want to use a power chair when I know you can walk a little bit yet?" more than ten times.
13. You have asked yourself the question, "Why do I want to

use a power chair when I can still walk a little bit yet?"
14. You realize the answer to the above question is, "Because I want to be able to walk a little bit for several more years and don't like the idea of ruining my arms/hands and ending up in a nursing home because I'm unable to care for myself."
15. You have to hide the keys to your scooter when you aren't using it, because the grandkids will take off in it, leaving you stranded while they run your battery down and stay just out of your reach.
16. All your clothes have shrunk two sizes since you got the wheelchair.
17. You can use exhaustion and/or inaccessibility as an excuse to get out of committee meetings.
18. You no longer do things on the spur of the moment because you have to plan how you will get there, how much energy you will have afterwards, how many days in bed the activity will cost you, and whether or not it's worth it (Ed. note: If it involves Tom Selleck or chocolate in any way, it is worth it)
19. Your grandchildren are holding your crutches hostage and will return them if you let them have the last chocolate chip cookie in the jar.
20. You try to find a way to crawl to the cookie jar before you give in and let them have that cookie.
21. You have dumped your cosmetics out of your make up case and use it to haul your pills around in. You figure your are better off feeling good than looking good.
22. You fall asleep as soon as your behind touches a solid surface.
23. You can't sleep at all, and the meditation tape you bought does not help. The sounds of crashing surf and gently lapping water only make you have to go to the bathroom.
24. You have more fun racing your wheelchair around in the mall than you ever did as a kid on a bike. Especially if you were never able to ride a bike. Especially if your parents wouldn't have let you ride the bike in the mall even if you could ride it.

25. Your spouse uses you and your wheelchair as a self-propelled wheelbarrow when bringing the groceries to the house.

Cabin Fever

December 10, 2001...I look out my patio door to see big, soft flakes drifting down as gently as, well, as snowflakes. Duh. I gaze into the night sky and am transported to a fairy land of white. It is beautiful and even better, it covers the mound of debris the contractor left when he built my ramp. I go to bed smiling, as the beautiful flakes conspire to keep me housebound for the next four months.

December 11, 2001...My grandkids are perfectly willing to shovel the snow off my ramp, but their idea of a perfectly shoveled ramp and mine vary widely. They are so chilled and have worked so hard, however, that I don't scold. It will melt off sooner or later and I'm tired from the long trip from which I have recently returned. A day or two in the house won't hurt me.

December 12, 2001...WHAT??? MORE SNOW!!! There is no possibility of my getting out the door. Dillon is willing to get my mail for me and I have plenty of groceries for now. This would be a good time to learn to pace myself, get some rest, recuperate from two months on the road. Maybe I can get some writing done.

December 24, 2001...All the kids made it for the traditional Christmas Eve supper. I am blissed out. I got pictures of all the grandkids who were here. Only one didn't make it. I got family pictures of each of my children and their wives and children. I also got a picture of me and my sons and of me and all but one of the grandchildren. The food was good, the kids were happy with their gifts, and I made out like a bandit myself. Life is good. Who needs to get out of the house anyhow?

January 20, 2001..It's nice that my family will help me with things like shoveling the snow off the ramp every other day, picking up groceries when I need them, but if I don't get out of this house soon, I am going to go stark staring sane. (Insane is no longer an option, been there, done that.)

February 19, 2001...Is that shiny thing in the sky the sun or a UFO? I chase the cat from her favorite spot in front of the patio door and absorb the sun myself. I allow the cat to sit on my lap, but she is huge and can't find room to roll, so she soon stalks off, tail lashing and muttering feline obscenities under her breath. I don't care...it's MY sunshine!!

March 1, 2001...Spring is only three weeks away. My ramp has remained snow-free for nearly a week. I even got in my van and went shopping, my eyes squinting in the sunshine like that darn ground hog seeing his shadow.

THEN AND NOW, NOW AND THEN

"Use it or lose it." "Conserve to preserve." We can't do both, so which is the right thing to do? When I had polio, way back in 1945, when dinosaurs roamed the earth, the first phrase was 'the' thing to do. We were told that if we didn't stop whining and do those painful exercises, wear the heavy braces, use the hated crutches, we would 'end up in a wheelchair.' That was frightening to a small four year old girl.

"Use it or lose it" worked very well. I could once again walk, albeit while wearing a full length brace of metal and leather that probably weighed nearly as much as I did. Small for my age, I struggled every morning to put on first the hated long stockings, then the ugly, heavy brace. No one heard me complain about it, with the possible exception of my younger sister, with whom I shared a room.

Then came the walk to school. It was ten long blocks in my hilly little town. No one thought it was too hard for me. Mothers, at that time, did not usually drive their kids to school. Indeed, if the family owned a car, Father was more than likely using it to get to work. Apparently, dinosaurs did not appreciate the sight of little girls in slacks, as they were not allowed in my school. So, when I took a shortcut one winter day and landed in a snowdrift up to my waist, I had to wait, shivering with the cold, till some older girls came by and could pull me out. There are few things colder, in my opinion, than a full length metal and leather brace that has been marinating in a snowdrift for half an hour or more. I did not complain about it. I doubt if I even mentioned it to my mother, who would not have been interested beyond scolding me for being so foolish as to get in such a situation.

Eventually, the brace was reduced to a below the knee orthotic. That was a relief. The short leg brace weighed roughly half what the other one did. So now I was expected to do even more. At age 10, I had surgery on my polio affected leg and left the brace behind forever. Or so I thought at the time.

Now there were no barriers to my doing everything anyone else did and doing it better than they did if at all possible. I took ballroom dancing lessons, I played baseball (with the boys fighting over who got to run for me in the unlikely event of my hitting the ball,) swam, roller skated, and as I entered high school, even more. I worked for 2 hrs. before and after school and during the noon hour, as a waitress. I played piano for the junior choir in my church and sang in the senior choir. I carried a full load of classes and maintained a straight A average. I was on the student council, the annual staff, and helped catalog the school's library of books. I was in band, both marching and concert, playing first clarinet. All the while hearing and believing my mother when she ranted at me for being lazy, clumsy, and ugly.

At age seventeen, I married a young farmer. We had three sons by the time I was 21. Since I couldn't drive a tractor (I'd figured out early on that if you could do something, that became your job and I had more than enough to do already) I got the 'easy' job of caring for the children of my husband's two brothers who farmed with him. Including my own three, that made ten. I also milked cows and took care of calves.

By the time I was forty, my husband had been diagnosed with cirrhosis of the liver. My father had Parkinsonism and Alzheimer at that time. My mother was furious with me, as usual, for not doing enough to help her. Dad had to go to a nursing home and Mom sold their house and moved to the apartments next door to the home.

I was babysitting again, this time with my grandchildren, from 5 AM till around 10 PM every day. None of my other workload had diminished because by now, my husband was very very ill and was often bedfast for weeks at a time.

I developed what may have been fibromyalgia. The doctor didn't know for sure what it was, but I would get muscle spasms around my chest that would cut off my breath, make my face and hands numb and my ribs would feel bruised when the spasm passed. I couldn't sleep, because lying down was excruciating.

My husband developed diabetes and refused to take any responsibility for his own care. So I monitored his blood, administered his injections, made his doctor's appointments, got his medications, cared for his every need. There would be long weeks of carrying every meal to him on a tray and then doing all the chores and all the housework as well. My sons helped as much as they could, but they were working. The burden was mostly mine.

Then, in the summer of '91, I broke my polio affected leg. Our sons rallied around and took care of the cattle. By this time the milk cows were long gone, replaced by purebred Angus cattle. I was unable to walk again for the next year and a half. When I did get back on my feet, I found I could no longer lift the brace I'd reacquired in my 40s. It took months of adjustments and new braces and finally qualifying for disability before I could resume my life.

Two years after my fall, my husband died. To fill the void, I went back to college and learned to use a computer. I went online and met a good friend from Canada and began to travel with her in '96. For the next four years, Carolann and I were inseparable. We traveled all over the US and Canada, camping in the van, either hers or mine, whichever one ran at the time.

In 2000, while visiting Carolann in her Ontario home, I met Jaan. We fell in love, slowly on my part, immediately on his. Three years later, we were married. I'd been a widow for 10 yrs. I'd dated a bit, but found the experience less than wonderful.

All this time, although I knew about Post Polio, I kept going at top speed. Slowing down was being saved for my old age. I wrote 4 books and self published them, I organized support groups, I did public speaking, I traveled. I enjoyed life very much. And I was in love with a tall handsome silver haired Canadian long haul trucker. He loved me, too. Life was good.

Alas, Poor Peasant

It's summer here in Saskatchewan and beautiful. In former days, I would look forward to family barbecues and picnics, but I don't do that now. For one thing, the family is nearly a thousand miles away, so it makes a longish commute. For another thing, I have, in my old age, discovered the death of my Inner Peasant. Do you have one of those?

She's the one who loves to camp, hike, cook over an open fire, chase children till they all drop in fatigue. I'm not sure my Inner Peasant hasn't always been at least comatose, if not terminal, but I do remember her on the farm, lugging sacks of seed corn and beans, feeding cows and nursing ailing calves back to health, caring for children, feeding hired men. Now, as I look closely into my own eyes in the mirror, I see her withered hulk lying in a corner of my mind, obviously no longer in working condition.

These days, I am a PPS Princess. PPS Princesses do not have to work till they are exhausted and have no more usable motor neurons. Now we have People Who Do That. We don't have to stagger behind a lawn mower, scrub floors or carry in groceries. Our People do that for us. I have a girl who takes care of my yard in summer and shovels snow in winter. I call Willow my Lawn Ornament/Snow Angel. Arlene comes in twice a month to shovel out the house, I mean do the heavy cleaning. I can also ask Arlene to drive me to my doctor's appointments. My friend Kathy and I go shopping once a week and she helps me carry in the results of the trip. Life is good for us PPS Princesses. Especially if you have a spouse who can pay for your People or one who is willing to, himself, be a People.

The problem is when I forget. Sometimes, my Inner Peasant stirs to life and tells me I can do this myself. And, of course, I can. It is difficult and I will pay dearly for it with debilitating fatigue, increased pain, and muscle spasms from You Know Where. But I can still do it. Then my Princess side gets into an argument with The Peasant and I get a bit down. Sometimes The Peasant wins, briefly, but in the end, I always come back to being a PPS Princess.

I think all of us with PPS are now Royalty. Let's try to remember that. It's so much easier to follow the Conserve to Preserve guidelines, if we just remember that Royalty does not have to do anything they don't enjoy. Let them eat cake

IT ALL DEPENDS ON HOW YOU LOOK AT IT

Alcohol is bad. Penicillin is good. No one will argue about that, I'm sure. Except...maybe me. While I am almost a teetotaler (a glass of wine with Christmas dinner doesn't count, does it?), I owe my existence to the presence of alcohol and the absence of penicillin.

We'll tackle the alcohol part first. My grandfather and grandmother were Germans from Russia. They lived near Odessa, on the Black Sea, in the Ukraine. Grandfather was not a teetotaler, apparently, because somehow, he had one too many and lost the keys to the granary of which he had charge. I 'm not sure exactly w hat happened after that, but it resulted in their borrowing some money from Grandmother's uncle Mike in South Dakota, leaving Russia and traveling to the New World.

Passage was booked on a ship going from Germany to the US. Grandfather, however, got thirsty on the way to the ship and one thing led to another. The ship left without my grandparents and their 5 children. They booked passage on the next ship, but had to come over steerage. I'm sure my grandmother's complaints were stifled when she found out that the first ship sank with no survivors. So. had Grandfather not tipped a few, 1 wouldn't be here.

Penicillin. My father's first wife died of pneumonia at the age of 28 or so because there was no penicillin. Had she lived,Dad would not have been available to marry my mother and, again, I would not be here.

This has brought me to the conclusion that nobody really knows for sure if the bad things that happen to us are truly bad and not a blessing in disguise. I believe it was Shakespeare who said, "There is nothing either good or bad but thinking makes it so."

My getting polio at the age of 4, the heavy brace and the difficulty in getting around seem like a bad thing. But they led to a spirit of self reliance. Every goal attained gave me more confidence. The cheering on of my family and of the small community where I grew up encouraged me to try ever harder.

Then I married, far too young, and had three sons in quick succession. At the age of 38, I was a grandmother. Too young!! Or was it? I didn't know about PPS then, and I had energy to spare. My oldest grandson, David benefited greatly from a young grandmother who would play with him, read to him, act out stories from Winnie the Pooh. Had I waited till I was older to marry, older to become a grandmother, the onset of PPS might have prevented a lot of this.

I was widowed at the age of 52. Was that a bad thing or a good thing? Both. I dearly loved my husband and I was lost without him. But, in filling that void, I went back to college and met some wonderful people, got on the Internet and met many more, did some traveling and eventually met Jaan, my present husband.

Through him, I've gained more friends, a loving and truly marvelous mother-in-law and even a new son. My children surely didn't expect me to present them with a 'baby' brother at my age! But I did. Of course, I missed out on this son's growing up years, but I am privileged to share his adult years. When things look black, remember this: It's the dark part of the tapestry that makes the golden threads woven through it show up more brightly.

You Can Do It

A group of us polio survivors were chatting the other day and talking about how difficult it was to ignore those old 'tapes' of what we were taught when we had polio. You know…keep on trying, try harder, push more, don't give up, don't whine, you can do anything if you put your mind to it.

Too many of us are still doing that…still trying to keep up with the Able-Bodied Joneses. And it is bankrupting us, in a sense, by causing us to spend motor neurons that we cannot spare.

Vicki said it had just dawned on her that we no longer have polio…we now have Post Polio, and they are NOT the same ailment. What worked so well to help us recover from polio just makes PPS worse. We must learn to reverse our thinking.

But if we don't do all the things we did before, we feel so guilty. I know I do. Maybe we should try to stand back and look at ourselves objectively…look at ourselves as if we were looking at a stranger. Would we ask another person to push himself or herself till he simply cannot move anymore? No, I don't think so. I think if we met someone who was in pain and was making it worse by overdoing, we'd tell that person to slow down, that they don't need to do all the things that seem so important. I believe we'd be far more compassionate to a complete stranger than we are to our own bodies.

I know I have no room to talk. I frequently give out exactly that advice and I have been known to say that any normal, sane, able bodied person would call in sick if he didn't feel well, but a polio survivor would go to work, dragging himself in on bloody stumps if necessary, just so no one would think he was a wimp or a cripple or, somehow, 'less than.' And then I go shopping with a girlfriend and don't take my travel scooter because it might inconvenience her. Or I cook a big meal for my able bodied family and insist on doing the dishes afterwards. Let's start treating ourselves as well as we would treat a complete stranger, at least!

DECISIONS, DECISIONS, DECISIONS

Making a decision about something takes me awhile. I like to take the idea apart, turn it over, check for cracks and booby traps, think of a best/worst case scenario, that sort of thing. It takes me about two weeks of solid thinking to make a major decision. That's where the PPS comes in. I can only do solid thinking for a few minutes a day and then my brain freezes up or wanders off and leaves no forwarding address.

Thus, it took me several months to decide to teach a class in Beginning Internet. I've talked to lots of people who mention they would love to know more about email and web surfing. I'm hoping they want to learn badly enough to pay me to teach them.

Now that I have definitely decided to do this, I've called the nearby elementary school and asked if I could use their computer lab. Yes, they said, if I do this class between 3:30 PM and 6:00 PM. That works out nicely as I expect my students to be mostly older people, retirees who, like me, prefer to spend their evenings in their pajamas watching TV or reading. A big bonus is that the school building is only about two blocks from my house.

Now, I have to decide what to teach exactly. Where to start, how far to go, will I be handing out homework assignments, stuff like that. More thinking. Can the polio dragon be bribed, perhaps with extra naps, into letting me function full steam for an hour or two twice a week? What exactly will I have to give up in order to have the energy to do this and do I want to do it that badly?

Will my students listen to me, or will there be some among them who adhere to the old thinking: your brain gets sucked out when you turn 50 and from then on, you are in permanent Duh mode? Worse yet, will they think their own brains got sucked out at age 50? I am confident I can disabuse them of both notions. If they are reluctant, I can always run over their toes with my chair.

Yes, I think I can do this. In fact, I'm sure I can. Maybe I'll have to give up a little housework in order to have enough time for a nap just before leaving for class. Oh, what a tragedy that would be, yes? Let me see...nerdling, my favorite occupation vs. washing dishes...hmmm...decisions, decisions, decisions.

FAREWELL TO OL' WONKY

Five years ago this month, I got my first power chair, a Jazzy 1105. It sat in the garage for a while, then got moved inside the house when the weather turned cold. I walked around it, warily, for another while. Finally, I got up the courage to use it. What a difference it made in my life. I hadn't realized how little fresh air I was getting. Since I couldn't walk any distance, I'd been going from my house to the car, from the car to the store, back to the car, back to the house. With the power chair, I could go to the post office and the bank in my small town and, on a nice evening or late afternoon, I could take a 'stroll' with my grandson.

Vocational Rehabilitation helped me get a Bruno Curbsider lift installed in the van that replaced my beloved little blue Sunbird. Now I had wings! I toodled all over town, went shopping, went to the zoo. It was wonderful. Later, Easter Seals and Vocational Rehabilitation put a long, long ramp on the side of my house. That really made my life easy.

Five years later, however, the power chair was starting to show its age. Its tires were balding. They don't make Rogaine for tires. The bearings were full of metal filings. The motors had developed a decided limp, appropriate for a polio survivor, but not very handy. Originally, the 1105 was supposed to fold so that it could be carried in the trunk of a car. Like that could happen. The lightest piece of this thing weighed in excess of 50 lbs. It did fold, but only while I was riding it, at which time it would spit its batteries onto the sidewalk. This necessitated someone (not me) getting down on hands and knees and replacing the batteries. The solution that was applied for this was to weld the frame solid. Unfortunately, not straight, but very solid. My tires now canted inward like a racing chair. And, best of all, the control lever went bananas.

Ol' Wonky, as I now called the 1105, would shy at a blown leaf like an unbroken horse and lurch sideways. Once it pinned the

Yes, I think I can do this. In fact, I'm sure I can. Maybe I'll have to give up a little housework in order to have enough time for a nap just before leaving for class. Oh, what a tragedy that would be, yes? Let me see...nerdling, my favorite occupation vs. washing dishes...hmmm...decisions, decisions, decisions.

FAREWELL TO OL' WONKY

Five years ago this month, I got my first power chair, a Jazzy 1105. It sat in the garage for a while, then got moved inside the house when the weather turned cold. I walked around it, warily, for another while. Finally, I got up the courage to use it. What a difference it made in my life. I hadn't realized how little fresh air I was getting. Since I couldn't walk any distance, I'd been going from my house to the car, from the car to the store, back to the car, back to the house. With the power chair, I could go to the post office and the bank in my small town and, on a nice evening or late afternoon, I could take a 'stroll' with my grandson.

Vocational Rehabilitation helped me get a Bruno Curbsider lift installed in the van that replaced my beloved little blue Sunbird. Now I had wings! I toodled all over town, went shopping, went to the zoo. It was wonderful. Later, Easter Seals and Vocational Rehabilitation put a long, long ramp on the side of my house. That really made my life easy.

Five years later, however, the power chair was starting to show its age. Its tires were balding. They don't make Rogaine for tires. The bearings were full of metal filings. The motors had developed a decided limp, appropriate for a polio survivor, but not very handy. Originally, the 1105 was supposed to fold so that it could be carried in the trunk of a car. Like that could happen. The lightest piece of this thing weighed in excess of 50 lbs. It did fold, but only while I was riding it, at which time it would spit its batteries onto the sidewalk. This necessitated someone (not me) getting down on hands and knees and replacing the batteries. The solution that was applied for this was to weld the frame solid. Unfortunately, not straight, but very solid. My tires now canted inward like a racing chair. And, best of all, the control lever went bananas.

Ol' Wonky, as I now called the 1105, would shy at a blown leaf like an unbroken horse and lurch sideways. Once it pinned the toe of my left shoe against the railing on the ramp. Thank goodness, that foot doesn't go all the way to the toe of the shoe, being several sizes smaller than my other foot. No harm done. Had it been the right foot, though, I would probably have broken a toe.

I talked to my family doctor about getting Ol' Wonky replaced before I broke something I might want to use later. Since I accidentally tore his plastic file holder completely off the wall and broke a chunk out of his examining table while I was getting the chair into the examining room, he knew I wasn't kidding. He very graciously told me that the file holder was ugly and would I mind going into all of the other rooms and wrecking the rest of them, too, so they could be replaced with something more attractive. Now that is tact!

My new Jazzy 1103 sits in blue splendor in my kitchen, even as we speak. It is sleek and shiny, has a joystick that wouldn't dream of wrecking Dr. Woolen's office, and rides like a Cadillac. It turns on a dime. So far, I have not scraped the arms up on my walls/doorways. (One friend of mine looked at the arms of Ol' Wonky and remarked that our hallways must be painted the same color. Her armrests bore streaks of Country White, too.)

I thank you, Dr. Woolen, for your hard work in getting me the new chair. My toes thank you, too.

HONK HONK HONK

Is that the sound of Canadian geese flying over? Is spring on its way? No, sadly, it is not geese. It's me. I have a heavy cold. I honk my nose often and loudly in order to breathe. It all started when my grandgerm...er...grandson visited and shared his cold with me. Always a generous soul, Dillon gave me a doozy.

The first day was not bad. A bit sniffly, a little bit achy. The second day, I slept all day. I couldn't get myself out of bed. The day drifted by in a fog of sniffly drowsiness.

The third day, my body reminded me forcefully of why I am on disability. My back objects violently to my lying down for extended periods. So, the third day was spent with back spasms, spasms in my midriff occurring when I tried to stretch out the spasms in my back and then the back reciprocating when I tried to straighten out the midriff spasms. I was miserable. I am on no pain medication at all, preferring to suffer my usually fairly mild pain levels rather than become a zombie. I overreact to pain meds and hate that groggy, undead feeling. I whined to Jaan. That is my pain relief of choice. I maintain that if you whine to someone who loves you enough to listen, the pain is spread out and is thus thinner. It works for me. Usually. Not this time.

I called my sister. "Do you think those pills for premenstrual cramps would work to relieve back spasms?" I asked her. "Worth a shot," she replied, and promised to bring me some. Unfortunately, when she arrived, she had Motrin, not Midol. "Oh," she said, disgusted with herself. "I just saw the big 'M' and thought I had the right thing!" Teasingly, I said I was glad she hadn't seen that 'M' on a Michelin tire and we both had a good laugh.

Not having had any sleep the night before because of the aforementioned spasms, I downed two more Valerian Root capsules. Usually one of these is just right. It smooths out my brain waves and lets me drift right off to sleep. I'd taken two the night before, to no avail whatever. However, this time, the Valerian Root worked. I slept well, but awoke groggy and lightheaded.

By this time, I realized that something absolutely had to be done to prevent those spasms returning.

Unable to drive or even to stay awake, my choices were limited. I settled on a heating pad. And I do mean settled. I applied the heat to my back as I curled up on the couch. I slept for a couple more hours. That day passed in a blur, too. I got up long enough to feed myself and back down. I used up all the Kleenex in the house. On my bedside stand, within easy reach, I kept a roll of toilet paper.

This is day six. My nose, while not as impressive as Arafat's, gives off a substantial glow that could be seen a long way across the desert. I carry my roll of toilet paper wherever I go in the house. I honk, therefore I am.

THERE IS ALWAYS SOMEONE WORSE OFF

How many times have you heard that phrase? "Don't whine because you have fallen down and skinned your knees again. Look around you and see how many people are worse off than you are!"

I think this was almost a mantra when I was growing up. I was never to ask for help, never to complain about the pain of the Physical Terrorist, never to have a sad or blue moment. Why not? Other people could, but I was always told, "There are lots of people worse off than you are! When you complain, it makes other people feel bad."

That was the Polio Way. Now that I'm older and can do as I like, I have begun to question this idea. Could this be why so many of us polio survivors grit our teeth and endure when we should be pacing ourselves, resting when needed, and refusing to do things that we know will exhaust us? I've always said that if an able bodied person broke a fingernail and could get away with calling in sick, he probably would. A polio survivor, however, would drag his body to work on bleeding stumps if he thought the alternative was people thinking he was lazy.

We've all been indoctrinated as children about not being helpless. We've been taught to try our hardest to be perceived as 'normal.' I am not advocating self-pity. I'm just suggesting that our pains just might be real and that it is irrelevant if someone else is hurting, too. If two people sit side by side and someone shoots at them, killing one and wounding the other, is the wounded one not still wounded? Yes, he's better off than the dead one, but his wound still needs tending. He is still hurt.
It may not be easy to break out of the Polio Mold, but I think we should at least try. I endured a lot of pain recently when my sciatic nerve became pinched. Did I go to a doctor? No. Lots of people were worse off than I was. I could still hobble around if I

gritted my teeth and groaned a lot. I shouldn't bother the doctor with my piddly little pains. Of course, I was thinking the pain was from PPS. I belong to several online polio groups and most of the people on them have a lot more pain than I do. I wasn't going to wimp out.

Finally a friend of mine who had not had polio and so could see things a bit more clearly told me she thought it was sciatica. She recommended a fellow who, while not licensed, was very good at manipulating the body and could, she was sure, release this nerve and help me. I reluctantly agreed to see him. Guess what. It wasn't PPS pain, it was a pinched nerve. He helped me enormously.

Even though several of my friends are battling worse pains than I am, my nerve was still pinched and all the empathy in the world did not help that pain. Just because someone else hurts, your pain is not irrelevant. It still hurts. It still needs to be dealt with.

Besides, I still think if you whine to someone you love, it spreads the pain around, making it thinner and easier to handle. It works for me!

Made in United States
Orlando, FL
27 May 2024